PUBLIC JESUS

PUBLIC JESUS

Exposing the Nature of God
in Your Community

TIM SUTTLE

the HOUSE studio

The House Studio
PO Box 419527
Kansas City, MO 64141

Copyright 2012 by Tim Suttle

ISBN 978-0-8341-2769-2

Printed in the United States of America

Editor: Kristen Allen

Cover Design: Arthur Cherry
Interior Design: Sharon Page

www.thehousestudio.com

10 9 8 7 6 5 4 3 2 1

With respect and admiration,
I dedicate this book to
the people of Redemption Church.

CONTENTS

ACKNOWLEDGMENTS

With a grateful heart I send my love and thanks to:

Kristin: I'd be lost without you. Here's to fifteen more years. Nicholas and Lewis: Further up and further in, boys! Chris Folmsbee: For asking me to do this project. Kristen Allen: Editor extraordinaire. Eddie Garlich: For being a great conversationalist. Ryan Cork: For lending your unique ability to be excited. AMO Fellows: For your friendship. TRG: For those enjoyable hours of extraordinary conversation. Redemption Church staff and elders: For believing it's possible to do serious theological reflection in the context of the local church. The people of Redemption Church: For holding nothing back. My family: For the heritage of faith, hope, and love.

INTRODUCTION

What role should our faith play in public life? Many people, even devout Christians, have been raised to believe that religion is personal and private, and therefore must be kept out of public life altogether. I was raised to think this way, and chances, are many of you were as well.

On several occasions over the years, when I have wanted to bring Jesus into public life, I've been reminded by a number of different Christians that Jesus once said, "My kingdom is not of this world." The Greek word translated "of" in this instance is *ek*, which is about a thing's origin: *ek* actually means more like "out of" or "from," so a more accurate reading of this passage would be, "My kingdom is not *from* this world."[1] While Jesus's kingdom is not *from* this world, it most certainly extends *to* this world and is most certainly *for* this world.

Even if we wanted to follow the dictum "religion is personal and private," doing so would be impossible. As the psalmist wrote, "The earth is the LORD's, and everything in it, the world and all who live in it" (Psalm 24:1). God belongs in the public square because the public square belongs to God. God is not only the one we pray to in the privacy of our own homes, but God is out and about in cultures and societies, working in every corner of creation to bring about God's good purposes.

God is public and God cares about public life. Yet, what it means for us to say that God belongs in public life is far from clear. Is it the street preacher shouting on the corner about the coming judgment? Is it backing Christian candidates for public office? Is it relief efforts, fundraising, Christian music, books, and concerts? How does God expect to be present in public life? What if the answer is as varied as the number of humans on the planet? What if the way God is present in public life is through you and me?

In the Beginning

In the beginning the Spirit of the Lord hovered over the face of the waters. In the Hebrew imagination, water embodied the theme of *chaos*. So, when it shows up in the Scriptures, water often represents the threat of chaos amid the purposes of God. When the disciples were in their little boat struggling against a powerful storm on the Sea of Galilee, they were not merely facing a storm. They were engaging the powers of chaos, which threatened the mission of God. When Jesus calmed the sea or walked upon the waters, he was demonstrating God's sovereignty over the chaos.

Chaos, the Bible teaches, will not reign forever. From the beginning of time, the master of the universe has been ordering the chaos. The entire creation story is about God ordering things: calling forth light from darkness, distinguishing day from night, separating land from sea, creating structure out of chaos. God has always been trying to bring right order to the world, and when it happens, God calls it "good." God's determination that creation should be rightly ordered involves not only each person, but also societies and cultures. It involves personal life to be sure, but it also involves public space.

How we order the chaos in our own lives depends upon what we believe about God. The Christian story tells us that within each individual, and within the heart of all communities, there exists a God-given drive to participate in the ordering of creation. Where we have failed to bring proper order to the world, chaos has reigned. Where chaos reigns, the powerful and the violent will almost always win out while many people suffer. So, part of our calling as children of God is to attempt to organize our world so that chaos doesn't reign in public life.

Living in the way of Jesus cannot be merely a personal, private thing because faith is meant to impact every aspect of life. God cares about all of life. I cannot check my faith at the door when I go into the super-market, drive my car, pay my taxes, give to a charity, volunteer, cash my paycheck, or vote. Everything I do in my life—be it private or public—is meant to be informed by my most basic identity: I am a follower of Jesus Christ, a Christian. When I live in faithfulness to Jesus as I navigate public space, I believe that I am participating in the deep and seminal reality that God is trying to bring right order to the world. My faith in Jesus must impact all that I say and do when I inhabit public space.

Granted, as we will see, there are pitfalls and ditches to public faith on either side of the road. The most common ditches people can get stuck in from time to time are named *secularism* and *fundamentalism*. Both are rigid doctrines based upon either/or thinking. Both attempt to bring order to the chaos by annihilating the other. In the end, both have failed to bring right order to our public life. Ironically, the way to avoid each ditch is not to straddle the fence between them—to somehow practice each in moderation—but to find a completely different option, a third way that transcends them both. This third way is called the gospel.

The gospel is the good news about how, through Jesus Christ, God calls and constitutes a people who will enter into relationship with him and be transformed by him, so that they can live and move in the world in such a way that they will anticipate how things will one day be when Christ comes again. Christians believe God has promised there will be a day in the future when sin, decay, and death will be dealt with once and for all. Evil will be stopped. The gospel tells us that this day—this future—has come rushing back into the present day through the life, teaching, death, and resurrection of Jesus Christ. Those who find their being in Christ can actually live in the present day as a kind of "early edition" of what the rest of the world will be like when God is finished with his redemptive project and Christ returns.

The five-dollar word for this is *prolepsis*: it means "to anticipate." What the church does in the present day is "proleptically actualize" the kingdom of God. We anticipate the age to come by the way we live together right now. We don't wait for eternity to happen because we believe eternity has broken into time through Jesus Christ. Through Christ, in the power of the Holy Spirit, we can actually live like eternity…right now. We can live as though Jesus is the world's true Lord because we believe that he is! Our "normal" should be this: among the people of God, sin, death, and decay no longer rule our lives. In our common life—the new community or church—evil has no place!

The church is often called the *new community* or the *new humanity*. Christ has shown us a new way to be human. Through Christ we have become the first fruits of the new creation. Our first and most basic confession is that Jesus is Lord of all. So the burning question for the church is not "Who is the Lord of all the earth?" We know who the earth's true Lord is. We know who is in charge. The question is, "Why doesn't the earth look like God is in charge?"

What would the world be like if God were in charge?

The answer, or answers, to that question will determine how the church should organize our common life. We organize in such a way that we reflect the lordship of Jesus. We can ask this question because we believe Jesus *is* here and present among the people of God. Jesus is alive and working in our hearts, in our common life, in the life of the church, and even in the societies, cultures, organizations, and structures of the world.

The answer to that question also depends upon another question: "Which god?" As Christians, our answer is simple: the God who has been revealed to us in this Jesus of Nazareth, who lived, taught, died, and rose again so that we all might experience life as God meant it to be.

What would the world look like if God were in charge? It would look like Jesus.

In Jesus's day it looked as though Caesar and Herod were firmly in control of the earth. It's no different for us now. In our day it still seems as though the Caesars and Herods of our world are running the show. But our confession that "Jesus is Lord" defies this view of reality. Our conviction is that the lordship of Jesus Christ is absolute. Despite appearances, Jesus has in fact already been crowned Lord of all creation.

The church's gift to the world is that we live right now in such a way that we embody the coming kingdom. We model it. We bear witness to the lordship of Jesus as we allow eternity to determine how we live today and every day. It doesn't matter to us if it seems like the Caesars and Herods of the world are running the show. We know they are not. Jesus is the world's true Lord.

One of the more important words we can use to describe what we are doing in the world, especially in public life, is the word *mission*. Mission involves the way we structure our lives and the way we embrace our vocation as the caretakers of creation. Part of our mission is to organize our common life together in such a way that we image God to all creation. Mission involves not just spreading beliefs but living our lives—personally and communally—under the direction of Jesus Christ. Mission involves more than this, but never less.

The chapters and videos in *Public Jesus* represent an attempt to wrestle with all kinds of questions about what it would mean for us to live our lives as though we believe Jesus is Lord of all. What if we reject the popular notion that religion is simply a private thing between you and God, and bring our faith into public life? If we begin with the assumption that our faith belongs in public, then we can truly ask what kind of role it should play. How do we bear witness to the lordship of Jesus Christ in public? How can we live a public faith?

Answering these questions will require great imagination and ingenuity. It will require much more from all of us than we will be comfortable giving. It will require that we embrace Jesus's call to take up our cross and follow him.

Chapter 1

TO BE A HUMAN BEING IN THE WORLD

When we focus on the cross, which, I see the cross as the center of history—everything before was leading up to that: everything after that is emanating from there—this is the center of history. As Jesus is breathing his last breath, the veil in the temple tears from top to bottom. One of the ways I like to talk about that is God is now not stuck behind a curtain in the temple: he is on the loose in the world. So, part of what it means to be a Christian is to figure out what God is doing and join with that.

This becomes a way of life, not a belief system. So Christianity to me is not simply a matter of beliefs; it's a being thing—it's a new way to be a human being. So I think seeing Christianity as a belief system sells short what it is that God is trying to do. What it means to follow Jesus is that you hold nothing back: you follow with your feet.

So the way I often talk about it is I'll say that we're meant to organize our common life together in such a way that we "image God" to all creation. When people look at us they see past us, to the reality behind it, which is that God is the master of the universe. He's made everything. It's all his. We somehow get to play some integral role in his right ordering of creation—and this is what it means to be human.

So when we're asking the question what the world would look like if God were in charge, what would public space look like if God were in charge, you look at Jesus. If you want to understand what it means to be a human being, you look at Jesus. If you want to understand how to order our common life, how to enter into public space, we go to his teaching. We say, actually, this is it, and this is terribly impractical and makes absolutely no sense, and yet, it's exactly what we have to do and be.

One morning last winter I had just showed up at my office, and sat down at my desk to do my morning prayers, pray the Daily Office. I had my computer up, and I, for some reason I glanced over at my e-mail or maybe it made a noise that told me to look at it. In the subject line of this e-mail, it said, "URGENT PRAYER REQUEST." I was like, "Oh no, something bad has happened."

The e-mail said something like, "I just passed over this bridge, and I'm pretty sure I saw Wendy, this woman from our church, standing on the bridge with a woman who was about to jump off." And I remember thinking at the time that if God was gonna ever ask somebody to go stand on a bridge with some lady, it would be Wendy. She's this woman who lives with kind of a radical yes to the world. She's available: she has lived her life available to God. So, she had a broken foot. She had *just* broken her foot that week, and so she couldn't drive, and so her

husband, Tom, was taking her to work. They were going over
this bridge, and she happened to see the woman on the bridge
and just something looked off. She said, "Oh my gosh, Tom, she's
gonna jump! That lady's gonna jump! Turn around!" Tom, he was
watching traffic: he hadn't seen it, but he flipped the car around,
they went back, and she hops out, broken foot and all, jumps
over the guardrail, and goes over to this woman.

The woman, she can tell, she's distraught. By this time she's
climbed over the fence, she is on the outside of the fence. There's
nothing between her and rush hour traffic going underneath this
bridge. Wendy starts speaking to her, and the woman is crying,
obviously upset. So Wendy reaches her hands as far as she could
through the chain-link fence and starts grabbing ahold of her
clothing and saying, "You don't wanna do this." I mean, just
saying the things that we would say to someone who's about
to do this horrible thing. But what Wendy said that has always
stuck with me. . . . She said at one point the woman looked at
her and they locked eyes. She realized in that moment, "I just
have to maintain eye contact." She kept just saying words to her,
words of hope like, "You never know how things are gonna end
up. You don't wanna do this." And the woman was sharing a little
about what was going on, why she was in the state that she was
in, and Wendy's holding onto her, and they're locking eyes.

I remember at the time thinking, that's what it means to be
a Christian. It's that we lock eyes with the culture somehow.
However it is, we're just available. She was just driving to work.
She wasn't on the mission field. She's not a preacher. She was
driving to work and saw some woman in trouble, and she goes

and she locks eyes with her and she holds on and doesn't let her do this awful thing she's planning to do.

Finally, the police showed up and a fireman in a harness pulled the lady off the ledge. But I think what lasts with me from that story is this image of locking eyes with the culture. Somehow this is part of what it means to be a disciple. We're obligated, and so we grab ahold of people and lock eyes with them, and we try to speak words of hope. When the rest of the world speaks, or lives, desperation and meaningless and death and destruction and what does it all mean, we speak hope, we speak resurrection, and that this somehow changes reality.

COMMENTARY

You woke up in the world. That's how it all started for you.

You did not choose to wake up in the world. You did not mean to.

You did not generate your own existence. Nor did you plan it.

You simply woke up here. You came alive. One day, probably when you were very young, you realized you are indeed alive; you consciously named the awareness that you are living here in the world.

From the beginning of time, human beings have held this one essential reality in common—we know that we are alive and living in a world we did not make. From the moment when we each wake up in the world, every thought and word, every action and reaction, every interaction and observation, every prayer and sigh, every fear and triumph, every kiss and joyful embrace, every moment great and small is an attempt to reconcile ourselves to our own existence. We are here, and we are all trying to make sense of our own lives. Why did we wake up here? Who called us into being, and for what purpose?

Our lives comprise the living out of our answer to that one profound and inescapable question: Why did I wake up here in the world? Much human angst comes from a dark suspicion that we can never truly find out the answer to that question. At one time or another, most people wrestle with this nagging fear that we toil in vain, without any purpose, without any guide, without any way to understand what it all means.

Telling the Right Story

The conversation about the origin and meaning of human existence never stops, although many of us stop thinking about it long before the issue is decided for us personally. For those who carry on the conversation, there are many approaches from which to choose.

The scientist begins the discussion with a big bang. The primordial stew. Electrical charges create amino acids that give rise to ever-evolving forms of life, constantly increasing in complexity over billions of years.

The philosopher considers the nature of truth. What does it mean to be human? How do we know what we know? Philosophers trace the development of thought and meaning, typically ending in either a hopeless sense of meaninglessness or in a hedonistic self-gratification.

So what does the Christian say? Christians take a different tack. We have been taught to engage this discussion in a peculiar way. We tell a story.

It's an odd thing to do, I'll grant you. Nevertheless, it's what we've always done. We tell a story. It's an ancient story that came to us in the form of a poem—told and treasured, memorized and repeated across generations until finally it was written down in a book we call Genesis. This book contains our beginnings.

This story tells us that we did *not* just wake up in the world by accident. On the contrary, we awoke in a world that was created by God. This world is evidence that we are not meant to experience God in a vacuum, but we are meant to experience God here in the place in which we came to life, choking and gasping for air, crying out and struggling to survive, aching to make our time on the planet mean something.

The story tells us that all along the way our creator has been trying to teach us what it means to be human, and this is why we were created. The story can help us understand how we can all live in accordance with ultimate reality as God has imagined it, as God has created it.

And the story goes like this.

> *The Triune God is,*
> *has always been,*
> *and will always be.*
> *From the beginning of time,*
> *from before time began . . .*
> *God is.*

This God exists as three-ness in one-ness—a plurality that is one, which exists in a permanent, ecstatic outpouring of love.

One day this love found expression. Creation!

And the three-ness in one-ness said, "'Let us make humankind in our image, according to our likeness; and let them have dominion'" (Genesis 1:26, *NRSV*). That's how it started. Humanity was ordained with a certain privileged status among all the rest of creation. Humans were granted limited power and given limited responsibility to rule over the earth—to be God's image-bearing creatures.

Then the three-ness in one-ness said, "'Be fruitful and multiply, and fill the earth and subdue it'" (Genesis 1:28, *NRSV*). So that the image bearing didn't stop with the first two humans, we were asked to fill the entire planet with other image-bearing humans. We have been created with our own ability to create and to procreate.

Finally, God puts human beings in a garden "'to till it and keep it'" (Genesis 2:15, *NRSV*). The human job description includes a specific obligation to the planet: we are its *keepers*. Our dominion is never to be exploitative because part of imaging God involves the care of creation itself. We are stewards who work with the dirt, with all matter, for that matter, and to help it to bear the fruit that sustains life.

That's our story. Well, that's part of it, anyway.

Humans were endowed by our creator with our own creative potential to fill the earth and bring it under our leadership, to till it and keep it, to care for it, and to cause it to bear fruit. When we are looking for answers about where we came from, and why we are here, this is the story Christians have been taught to tell. *We are placed here in the midst of God's world in order to organize our common life together in such a way that we image God to all of creation.*

As we bear God's image in every corner of the planet, we will help all the earth fulfill its intended purpose. It's an enormous vocation, and God has given it to us collectively as a human race. This is what it means to be a human being in the world. You see, we are not simply meant to chase our dreams, accomplish our personal goals, or get what we want out of life. We are not a giant collection of autonomous individuals. A big part of what it means to be a human being in the world is that we are born of and into a community. It means that we are designed by the Triune God to live together in community, in a particular way. We are to relate to one another and to all of creation in such a way that when people look at us, they can see that the three-ness in one-ness stands behind all of it, sustaining it by sheer force of will.

Now, humans have struggled with this vocation to say the least. We have stories to tell about that as well.

> *Sin filled the garden.*
> *Then it filled the earth.*
> *The human race was broken.*

In the days of Noah, God decided to try to fix the broken cultures by destroying evil. So God found the one and only righteous human and stuck him in an ark with remnants of creation. The rest of the world would suffer annihilation. Like cosmic-chemotherapy. God would attempt to kill the disease before it killed the whole organism.

The problem was, Noah climbed off the ark, got drunk, and passed out . . . naked. The chemo was unsuccessful and God declared that the whole project was flawed. Noah was still marked by a profound inability to make it happen—to bear the image. So God put his bow on the ground with no arrow in it and said, "'I establish my covenant with you: Never again will all life be cut off by the waters of a flood; never again will there be a flood to destroy the earth'" (Genesis 9:11). Ever since then we've continued to strive, to toil, to attempt to make a dent in the darkness.

Sometimes we've succeeded. More often than not we've failed to image God, and there are times when it can start to feel like there isn't any point in trying. But just when the time was right, something incredible happened. God entered in. What we could not do for ourselves, God decided to do for us.

This was good news for those who worried that the meaning of our existence would forever be just beyond our grasp. For those who began to fear we must have been left all alone to toil on the planet. For those who began to line up around their own agendas for how to bring the kingdom—holiness agendas, violence agendas, separatist agendas, and colluding-with-the-powers agendas—God entered in, as only God does, and started fixing it.

Jesus was God's personal address to us about what it means to be human. This is incredibly good news. God has not left us to suffer here by ourselves, struggling to make meaning out of a meaningless existence. God has come for us in Jesus Christ.

If we want to understand what it means to be human, ultimately, we look at Jesus Christ. Jesus keeps us from getting lost in endless observation with the scientist or endless supposition with the philosopher. Jesus draws us back into the story, helping us find the thread by connecting us to his mission of redemption.

Locking Eyes with the World

In the video I tell a story about my friend Wendy, who locked eyes with a woman who was about to jump off of an overpass into rush hour traffic on the freeway, and talked her down. I love this story. It's the locking eyes part that really gets to me. I think that I will never know a truer picture of what it means to be a Christian than my friend Wendy locking eyes with a woman who is on her last leg, desperate, and dying, literally.

Here's the thing. As Christians, we are called to lock eyes with the world each and every day.

The Sermon on the Mount from Matthew is the longest record of Jesus's teaching in existence. There he teaches with authority, explaining what it means to be a human being in the world. At one point he describes to his listeners what sort of impact they are supposed to have on public life. Eugene Peterson's Message version of this passage really brings the text to life.

> "Let me tell you why you are here. You're here to be salt-seasoning that brings out the God-flavors of this earth. If you lose your salti-ness, how will people taste godliness? You've lost your usefulness and will end up in the garbage. Here's another way to put it: You're here to be light, bringing out the God-colors in the world. God is not a secret to be kept. We're going *public* [my emphasis] with this, as *public* as a city on a hill. If I make you light-bearers, you don't

think I'm going to hide you under a bucket, do you? I'm putting you on a light stand. Now that I've put you there on a hilltop, on a light stand—shine! Keep open house; be generous with your lives. By opening up to others, you'll prompt people to open up with God, this generous Father in heaven." (Matthew 5:13-16, *MSG*)

In a way, this paragraph constitutes Jesus's updated teaching on the creation poem. "Let me tell you why you are here," he says, and he describes our vocation in new terms. We are to be salt and light—salt to bring out the God-flavors of the world and light to bring out the God-colors. Jesus came not merely to prepare our hearts for eternity, but to set eternity in our hearts so that we can walk around with it—shining like a light, tasting like salt—and work it into every aspect of our culture.

To be a Christian is not merely a "believing" thing: it is a "being" thing. When Jesus invited people into his way of being, he asked them to follow him into public space. Jesus was not about building the church. He was about building the kingdom through the church. The church is not the end in mind: the redemption of the world is.

"We're going public with this, as public as a city on a hill."

Our faith is public.

Jesus is public.

"Salt and light" is the kingdom-of-God-version, or the gospel-version, or the Jesus-version of the original vocation introduced way back in the Genesis narrative. *We organize our common life together in such a way that we image God to all creation*. We don't separate out into a Christian ghetto: we lock eyes with the world and shine a light into the darkness.

This is also part of what we are saying when we talk about "mission." Locking eyes with the world is about mission. Imaging God to the world is about mission. Our mission is to shine a light and bring out the God-colors. Our mission is to season the earth like salt and bring out the God-flavors.

When we organize our common life together in such a way that we shine like the light of the world, we will somehow be visibly, undeniably, rudely interrupting the world that has chosen to go its own way. The light emanates from a city, a community, not just individuals. The city on the hill shines and bears witness to all who are living in the valley of the shadow of death. The salt of the earth restores flavor for those whose life has become bitter and unbearable.

The life, teaching, death, and resurrection of Jesus Christ signal a seismic shift in the relationship between human beings and God. No longer is God stuck behind a veil in the temple. God is now on the loose and invading public space. And the church is the way God is now physically present to the world.

The church is to be the physical manifestation of the spiritual reality that Jesus is the world's true Lord. We are not simply content to be going to heaven when we die and to sit idly by while the world goes to hell in a handbasket. We are obligated by our vocation as God's image-bearing creatures to invade public space with the good news that Jesus is the world's true Lord.

DISCUSSION QUESTIONS

What is the very first memory you have? Do you remember realizing you were alive?

How often do you think about the meaning of your own existence? Do you ever worry that life has no meaning?

How do you lock eyes with the culture?

Is the vocation of being salt and light one that comes easily for you or with difficulty?

When you think of human vocation as bearing the image of God—being salt and light—do you find yourself resisting it, loving it, confused by it, worried by it, pressured by it, or something else?

Chapter 2

VOCATION: LEARNING TO COUNT THE RIGHT THINGS

I heard a story from a church planter one time. He was going to start this church and he'd invited all of his friends over to he and his wife's house, and they were just dreaming about what it was going to be like. His wife was sitting in the kitchen and they were talking and all of the sudden—he was going to be the lead pastor—all of the sudden his wife says, "I'm out! I'm not gonna do this!" And everyone thought she was joking at first, but she was serious. She said, "I'm out. I don't wanna do this." They said, "Why?" and she said, "You don't count what I do. What I do doesn't count."

What she did is run a company. She had a small business. She was pouring all of her energy into this small business, which is her passion. It's her job, which also helped to pay the bills. You know, behind every church planted is a spouse who pays the bills. So she said, "You won't count what I'm doing, and what I'm doing is providing income for families. I run my business like a family. We talk about our problems; we bear each other's burdens. I'm trying to be the hands and feet of Christ in this place, and you won't count what I do unless I can get them to come to church."

I think a big part of the problem, when it comes to our work life and our career, is that we don't know what to count. I read once, people will spend 65 percent of their waking hours at work. That is a *huge* part of our life that, if it is disconnected from the mission of God, what a waste! What a waste that 65 percent of our waking hours we would not count. That's a terrible injustice.

Part of my job is to teach people what to count. The point is to go into the world as the hands and feet of Christ as the body of Christ is salt and light. If 65 percent of our waking hours are spent at work and our religion is kept private—it's separate—then of course our jobs are toil. Of course we have trouble connecting what we do with the mission of God. I mean, I don't know how many times I have lunch with people in my congregation who say, "I just wish I could be in ministry." And you know, it only takes once, or maybe twice, to say, "You are in ministry: your job is your ministry, and we count what you do. It counts! In fact, what we do over here in this church is preparation for what you do over there." I wrote about this before—that the metaphor we use at my congregation for what the church is is the lungs. That we're breathed in every week, in this sacred space and time. Then we're breathed out into the culture to take those things out there. Then we're breathed back in. It's this constant weekly motion of breathing out, breathing in. Every once in a while, somebody else gets breathed back in with us. But for the most part that's not what happens: we're just breathed out into our workplace, our neighborhood, our families, our friendships. We take with them good news. We take with them the nutrients that we receive as part of the body of Christ.

I think that helps us view our work not as toil. You know, toil is mentioned in Genesis as a part of a judgment. Part of what Jesus is doing in our lives is to repair the breaches. I think what the resurrection tells us is toil is not how it has to be.

I'll often talk with folks about the difference between having a career and having a vocation. A career is what you do with your time. Our culture is very career focused. I think when we start to view our jobs as part of what it means to be Christian and we realize our vocation transcends career, whatever career you're in, your vocation is to image God in that place. So you become the hands and feet of God in that place. Whatever that means. So, you might be a doctor, you might be an accountant, you might be a mom who raises the kids and who takes care of the household. Those careers are different: the vocation is the same. You image God in that place. You make yourself available and then all of the sudden, it's not toil anymore. It's mission. It's not the soul-crushing job: every day is an opportunity to be good news in some place.

COMMENTARY

Have you ever had a soul-crushing job?

Do you have a soul-crushing job right now?

If you have to ask what a soul-crushing job is, you've never had one. A soul-crushing job is one that makes you dread getting up on Monday morning. It makes you feel like you are wasting your days here on earth. You feel fully alive from the moment you leave work on Friday until Sunday evening. The rest of the time, you are just getting by.

I've had several soul-crushing jobs. The worst was a job doing data entry. I sat at a desk all day and entered numbers into a computer from medical testing reports. I spent most of my days thinking, "Did I go to college for this?" I made some good friends and enjoyed the people I worked with, but getting up to go to work every day doing data entry was a grind. It was soul crushing.

When I was in college I had another soul-crushing job: school bus driver. The actual driving was okay, and the kids were usually fun, but what was soul crushing about the job was getting up at five thirty in the morning to go to work. Up at five thirty, classes all day, back to work at three o'clock, a second job some evenings, then homework and studying at night. I was miserable. I remember waking up and getting in the shower about the time many of my friends were just coming home. So many mornings I would stand in the shower and cry. I was just so tired and miserable. It was soul crushing.

A soul-crushing job can be toxic to your soul. Yet, we have to work. Human beings work. It's what we do. We are meant for it.

We work inside the home and outside the home. We work for cities and corporations. We work for ourselves and for others. Some people work to live: some people live to work. Work is a big deal in our culture as it is in every culture.

Some people love their jobs, which can be annoying, I'll grant you, but there it is. These people might describe their work as a soul-sustaining job. They actually look forward to going to work. For those whose work seems to be soul sustaining, for those who love to go to work each day, there seems to be an element of challenge in their work. Their work is difficult and demanding: it's part of what they love about it. It's hard, but it's worth it for some reason. Nothing beats soul-sustaining jobs. They can make our days joyful and fulfilling.

I'm now a pastor of a church, and I can honestly say that I have a soul-sustaining job. I get paid to study the Scriptures. I have to make myself stop working and attend to other important things like family, hobbies, and staying in shape. I sometimes feel like I'm more myself when I'm working really hard at my job than I've ever been before. I often feel a sense of God's pleasure in what I'm doing. I'm not alone, either. Many of my friends who are not employed by the church have the same sensation. When they work, they feel a sense of purpose and meaning. Some people have a soul-sustaining job. Some people actually love their job.

Maybe you are in a soul-crushing job that you hope will not last forever. Maybe you have a soul-sustaining job that is extremely demanding, but rewarding as well. Maybe you are somewhere in the middle. Wherever you are, we all have to find some kind of work to do because we are going to spend a good portion of our lives doing it. Is it too much to ask that our jobs would actually mean something?

There has to be more to life than a soul-crushing job.

Why it so hard to find a soul-sustaining job?

Is there such a thing as a theology of work?

The Story of Work

God is a worker. The story of work in the Bible begins with God doing all the work.

> In the beginning when God created the heavens and the earth, the earth was a formless void and darkness covered the face of the deep, while a wind from God swept over the face of the waters. Then God said, "Let there be light"; and there was light. And God saw that the light was good; and God separated the light from the darkness. God called the light Day, and the darkness he called Night. And there was evening and there was morning, the first day. (Genesis 1:1-5, *NRSV*)

> God works.
> God works through words.
> God speaks and it is so,
> and then God calls it "good."

There is a kind of freedom to God's working. God can create things however God wishes to, and it is simply all . . . good.

Part of God's work was to create humankind in God's image. As we explored in the Introduction, human beings were created with a specific vocation in mind. In the beginning our vocation was to be fruitful and multiply, fill the earth and subdue it, have dominion over it, till it and keep it, and help it to bear fruit. Our vocation is to fill the earth and organize our lives in such a way that we image God. This, as it turns out, takes a lot of work.

One of the essential elements of what it means to be a human being in the world is that we have been created to work. Work is meant to be a point of contact between God and us. Work is meant to be a connection for us: a source of meaning; a spiritual thing; a holy thing.

Does it sound strange to us that work should be a holy thing? God is a worker and we are workers because we bear the image of God—because "God said," and "it was so." Just as there is a freedom to God's work, there is meant to be a freedom in our work. Does your work seem like freedom? We are given dominion on the earth. We are granted some limited freedom to rule and organize the world. We are supposed to use this freedom to "till the earth and keep it." We are supposed to work alongside God to make the ground bring forth fruit and sustenance, and we are never supposed to exploit our freedom and dominion and harm the earth. We are put in charge of the world as God's agents and representatives.

We are told to till it.

We are told to keep it.

The word "till" in this passage from Genesis is the word *abad*. We know the word *abad* from the verse, "'As for me and my household, we will *abad* the Lord'" (Joshua 24:15). To till is to *abad*, or to serve. The word "keep" is the word *shamar*. We know *shamar* from the verse, "'[May] the Lord bless you and *shamar* you,'" (Numbers 6:24) or keep you. We are to serve the earth. We are obligated to serve and care for creation. We are meant to keep the earth.

Soul-crushing jobs very often have some element of the work that is exploiting creation instead of keeping it. Often our jobs are so disconnected from creation that it becomes hard to connect the dots between what we do and caring for creation. Often there is some sense in which a soul-crushing job is exploiting the earth instead of keeping it.

Part of the story of work in the Scriptures is that humans are given some freedom. The first family was told they were allowed to eat from every tree in the garden except for one. "'Of the tree of the knowledge of good and evil you shall not eat, for in the day that you eat of it you shall surely die'" (Genesis 2:17, *ESV*). They were free to eat from nearly everything, with one exception. From the beginning, humans have been asked to recognize that there are limits to our freedom. We are asked not to choose to work in such a way that we exploit creation and harm it and ourselves in the process.

Freedom can be abused. And it was. The first humans went on to harvest in illegitimate ways. They consumed in illegitimate ways. From that moment on, God said that everything was going to be harder now. The ground will begin to work against us. It will bring forth thorns and thistles. And work will have a new name. *Toil.* After creation, the ground doesn't do what we want it to do. Creation doesn't act how it is supposed to act. Something is off at a very base level. Everything we are meant to do and be as human beings has become more difficult. God said to Adam,

"Cursed is the ground because of you; through painful toil you will eat of it all the days of your life. It will produce thorns and thistles for you, and you will eat the plants of the field. By the sweat of your brow you will eat your food until you return to the ground, since from it you were taken; for dust you are and to dust you will return." (Genesis 3:17-19)

Enter the soul-crushing job.

Redeeming Work As Vocation

Do you think of the workday as something to just get through? Do you work just to get to the end of the day so you can do the things you really want to do? Is work just another name for toil?

When we see work as toil, life begins to lose the sense of freedom and joy for which it was created. If we experience our job as something we have to endure, and we do this day after day for 65 percent of our waking hours, for the rest of our lives, then how will our lives be sweet? When work is toil, we are no longer free. We become like slaves. Work becomes something warped and twisted, and our entire lives can become this way as well. It's as though we're not only trying to get through the day: we're actually trying to just get through our life to the good stuff at the end.

Toil devalues life.

Toil is a distorted view of work.

Redeeming a healthy sense of work is not easy. On this side of the fall, the ground just seems to work against us. However, Christians are supposed to be living into the reality that Jesus is Lord. We are meant to live each day as though eternity has broken into time. We have been created to organize our lives so that we image God, so that we become salt and light. We cannot do this if we spend 65 percent of our lives in a soul-crushing job!

Many of us cannot easily change our work situation. So, how can our jobs—the ones we have right now—be transformed from soul-crushing jobs to soul-sustaining jobs? How can our work be transformed from toil to vocation? Is it possible that Jesus could give us a way to approach our work in such a way that it will not do harm to our souls? Is there a way to work that will allow us to delight in work and worship God through our work?

I heard a story once about two men who worked in a marble quarry. The first man was asked about his work. He said,

> This is the most miserable job I've ever had. All I do all day is make big rocks into smaller rocks. No matter how much I do, I never accomplish anything. There are always more rocks. I'm miserable from the moment I get up until I lie down.

When the second man was asked about his work, he said,

> I have the best job in the world. I get to come out here in the forest to work. I take this raw stone, worthless and ugly, and I harvest it and send it off to be cut and polished. My work will end up being on display in some of the most amazing places in the world. It will be seen by millions. It will be walked on by kings and presidents and popes and bishops, and even by the poor pilgrim hoping to see the face of God. I'm so happy in this job. I can't wait to come to work.

They were doing the same job!

To one it was toil. To the other it was holy.

One man was a slave. The other was free.

One was miserable. The other was joyful.

Sometimes the choice of whether we have a soul-crushing job or a soul-sustaining job is just that simple: it's up to you. What do you want? Sometimes the only way to cease becoming a slave is to realize you have already been set free.

Part of what it means to be free in Christ is to no longer fear the grave. We no longer fear the ground as our final resting place because we believe in resurrection. If death doesn't have the final word in the end, then why should it have the final word right now? Maybe we can live resurrection lives. Maybe we can do resurrection work. Maybe we can work in a new creation way right now, even though the ground still bears the curse. Sure, the systems of the world are fallen. The economic, legal, educational, political, and social systems of the world are not the way they are supposed to be. The ground still bears the curse. Maybe, though, it's possible to work as though we are free because we do not fear the ground.

The story of work isn't just about how things are supposed to be but aren't. It's not just about the fall of creation, but the redemption of it as well. It's not just a story of where we came from, but a story about what is now possible through Jesus. Our work can become a part of the mission of God.

If Jesus is making all things new, then Jesus is making our vocational life new.

Work As Worship

When we read the Genesis account of the creation of earth and sky, sun and moon, the story is not just an account of where the sun came from. Because the sun still has work to do.

Ninety-nine percent of all of the energy available in the world comes from the sun. Through photosynthesis the sun's energy is converted into plant life. Plant life draws nutrients from the soil and converts carbon dioxide to the oxygen, which fills the atmosphere so animals can live. Plants feed the animals. Animals fertilize the soil. The soil grows more plants.

If you trace energy back through the food chain, what you'll find is that in the beginning, God created the sun with work to do. The sun's work is to shine and give off energy. The plant's work is to convert that energy into life. The animals eat the plant life and on it goes. All of it is connected from the largest thing to the smallest.

God created humans out of the dust of the earth. We are made of earth. To this day, every cell in our body comes from the earth: the soil, the water, the plants and animals we eat are all sustained from the soil. All that we are is connected back to the dust of the earth.

The story of creation isn't just about how things came to be. The story of creation is about how they are meant to work together. We will find meaning in our work only when we begin to understand ourselves as part of the whole. Work, in the beginning, was meant to find its meaning and purpose in the web of life. Whatever our hands find to do is somehow connected to everything that is.

Our work will find meaning when it becomes connected to the web of life. Work finds purpose when we understand how it is connected to that original vocation to till and keep the earth, to have dominion over creation. Our jobs, our work will have meaning for us only when it finds its proper place in God's good creation. And when it happens, work becomes worship.

Do we have careers that are worship? Or do we worship our careers? Do we care more about our careers than we do about doing work? Careers are self-focused: work or vocation is world-focused. Careerism is just a way of worshipping our work so that it no longer feels like toil and slavery. The Christian vocation is meant to transcend profession or career.

We live in a culture that has a false hierarchy of profession. For example, try to rank the following jobs: plumber and doctor. Without some sort of criteria, most people will rank doctor above plumber. The Christian view of profession is that these are actually both equally important careers. Both careers are the same because in each the vocation is the same—till the earth and keep it. You can see this by simply connecting each one back to its rootedness in the web of life. Since the advent of modern medicine— antibiotics, aseptic operating rooms, pain medicine, chemotherapy, and on and on—do you know what the most important advance was, the one that has fought more disease over the past four centuries than anything else? The answer is clean water and safe, reliable sewers. Over the past four hundred years, plumbers have done more to stop disease than doctors. Give it up for the plumbers.

When work is reduced to careerism, its divine dimension is cut off and God's intention for work is distorted and twisted. Work becomes like slavery when it's supposed to be about freedom.

Everything we do is meant to be an act of worship. Our jobs are a way of worshipping God. If we image God in the workplace, then our work is mission. If we do our work as though we are playing our small part in the redemption of the cosmos, then our work is mission. We are not meant to merely endure work because our work—when it is drawn up into the mission of God—has meaning and purpose. What we do in our jobs can connect to the new creation somehow.

DISCUSSION QUESTIONS

Have you ever had a soul-crushing job?

> Have you ever had a soul-sustaining job?

Spend some time connecting the dots between what you do and the web of life. How does what you do serve society?

> Is there ever a time when our jobs are causing harm to the creation and we should stop or find a new career? How will we know if this is the case for us?

Chapter 3
SABBATH:
AT PLAY IN THE WORLD OF PLENTY

I heard a guy once at a conference—I think he was a "life coach." He was talking about pace of life, and I was just reminded that healthy things go like this, right? [Moves finger slowly up and down multiple times as if to emulate a heart monitor.] This is healthy. So this is your breathing. This is what a heartbeat looks like. This is what life looks like. And yet *this* [moves finger in a straight line from bottom left to top right] is what business looks like. It's a straight line up and to the right. If this is living stuff [wavy finger movement], *this* [straight finger movement] is dead stuff. This is flatlining, right? I think we live in a world that pushes up and to the right, and that's just not life: that's death. In a culture that pushes everything up and to the right, a people that go like this [wavy finger movement] are amazing.

I have this friend who is an extreme athlete. He competes in Ironman triathlons—the big ones. And he was training for a trail race: they run these trail races that are twenty-four-hour races. You compete with a team of guys. I mean, these guys are crazy athletes. He was training for this here in Johnson County in Kansas City. What he was doing to train was getting up in the middle of the night and throwing like canned goods and heavy stuff in a backpack, and running down Shawnee Mission Parkway. It's this big, huge four-lane road with a median in the center with grass. He was running, to simulate a trail, in the middle of the night to simulate this twenty-four hour deal. A cop pulls him over and asks, "What are you doing?" He's sitting there with his backpack on having run for two hours. He's got a headlamp on, you know, lighting his way. The cop's like, "What are you doing?" He explained, and the cop just goes, "Go home. *Go home.* Stop, turn around, and go home. This is not acceptable behavior."

I've always thought of that when I think about Sabbath and what a radical thing Sabbath is. If you try to readjust our culture's relationship with time, the culture will push back just like a policeman saying, "Go home. You can't run down Shawnee Mission Parkway in the middle of the night with a headlamp on and a backpack full of canned goods. Okay? Go home!"

I think we live Sabbath as a witness to our culture that you can't go like this [straight finger movement] and live. Your life has to move like this [wavy finger movement]. There is evening. There is morning. This is a day. We work, we sleep, we spend time with our family. This is a day. Part of the week is work, and this day is rest.

When I was a kid, I grew up going to church every week, and my mom would—while we were doing our Sunday school lesson and memory verse before we left for church—my mom would make dinner. She would put it in the oven and set the timer. We would go to church and we would come home, the meal would be baked, so you would walk in the door with all those smells. You sit down to this Sunday dinner. (You know, we don't do the Sunday dinner anymore.) We'd do this big dinner and we'd all eat till we were full. Then there was this period of time between when we finished the meal and when we went to clean up the mess.

That time, the Hebrew people call *Menuha*. It's this sacred time where you just sit there and just delight in this feeling of being full. You don't want to be the first one to get up and start cleaning up the dishes. You want this sacred moment, this *Menuha*, to last, where you just delight in the delectability of the moment. Just be present and visit and talk and laugh and be together. That's Sabbath. It's not a laborious cessation of work. It's not an obligation. It's this sacred opportunity to realize we have enough. We have been taken care of—that life is good.

I think often we think of the Sabbath as the cessation of work. But it's more like the cessation of restlessness. It's the one day a week where we stop generating our life and we start receiving life. It's meant to be freedom from this anxiety and this rush that we're all in. It's meant to be this joyous celebration that God is the God of enough. That everything we have we need. If we're present in the moment we can linger in that place all day long.

If we do this in front of a world that's moving up and to the right, it is a radical public proclamation of good news. It's a very public thing to observe Sabbath, and it's an important part of bearing witness to the good news.

COMMENTARY

Time is a building block of culture. It says things about who we are.

Time is like language. It speaks.

The way we arrange our lives in relation to time tells us about who we are as a people. We are socialized to respect certain norms with regard to time. A new day starts at midnight. A workweek is forty hours. A night's sleep is eight hours. A sitcom lasts thirty minutes. If you go outside the norms, the culture will attempt to correct you in some fashion.

There is a man who lives in my neighborhood who works at night and sleeps during the day. We have a fairly busy street, and there are often people knocking on doors. Postal workers, FedEx, UPS, Girl Scouts, school kids doing fundraisers—it's a busy place on some days. This man has signs posted on his door declaring he's a day-sleeper. He installed a hinged cover on his doorbell to make people think twice before ringing. At one point he even wrote, "I sleep during the day" in white shoe polish on the back window of his car, which sits in front of his house. People still wake him all the time.

If you deviate from the social norms with regard to time, then you are attempting to reshape or renegotiate who we are as a society, and the society will continually challenge you.

Everything We Do Shapes Us

If time is a building block of our society, it is also a building block of the person. How you spend your time will shape who you are becoming. In the suburbs where I live, nine out of ten times, I greet somebody with the question, "How are you doing?" Often, the answer I'll get back is, "I'm so busy!" Think about that response for a moment. "Busy" has become the answer to a question concerning the quality of our lives. This is not good.

This answer does not come from out of the blue. We've been trained to give this answer by our culture and by the way we relate to time. In large part we pursue busyness because we've been taught that busy = important. If you have too much available time, you just aren't trying hard enough. You are on the edge of irrelevance. If you are not busy, you are not important, or so says our society. But we know something different. We know that unchecked busyness actually deforms people and societies.

If you've ever spent any time in a gym or exercise facility, then you have probably seen this guy. He's always in the weight room, usually grunting loudly and sweating profusely. He's the guy who has an incredibly overde-veloped upper body—his arms, chest, and shoulders are huge—but he has tiny bird legs. That's Western life. We are really busy: we all think we are important, but in truth we lack depth, stability, and real strength. We have no foundation that will help to guide our relationship with time.

Sabbath is meant to be the foundational structure of our relationship with time. Psalm 127:1-2 says,

> Unless the LORD builds the house, its builders labor in vain. Unless the LORD watches over the city, the watchmen stand guard in vain. In vain you rise early and stay up late, toiling for food to eat—for [God] grants rest to those he loves.

The psalmist teaches that busyness is an exercise in vanity. Rest, on the other hand, is connected to the love and goodness of God. Sabbath rest is evidence of the love of God.

Sadly, most people's relationship with time has become so warped by busyness that they can no longer find rest. The best they can hope for is to find a diversion. This is part of why our culture is so hooked on television. What most people need to do is rest. What they do instead is watch television. Scientists who have studied the way the brain reacts to television have taught us that the left brain shuts off almost immediately. The left brain is the calculating part of the brain. At the same time the right brain turns on, but at a very low, almost semi-conscious level. Then it begins to release endorphins, which make us feel very relaxed and pleasant. The net effect is that we enter a sort of trance-like state in which we are highly susceptible to suggestion, which is probably why advertising works so well.

Television is not the same as rest. At best, television is a diversion. At worst, it's voluntary brainwashing. Yet, television has taken on almost a religious element in our culture. We are faithful to television. We are devoted to it. We worship it with our time and our treasure. We allow it to exercise a religious-like power over our culture. Television—the ultimate diversion—has replaced Sabbath in American culture.

Father Adam Ryan is a monk at Conception Abbey and has been my spiritual director for many years. Father Adam once told me that if I were smart, I would stop at Walmart on the way home from the abbey and buy a shotgun. Then I would go home and take every television out of the house into the backyard and shoot them with the shotgun. Then I would take the gun to the police to have it destroyed. Father Adam said, "If you do this, you'll have a better relationship with your family, and you will have done two good deeds that day."

Maybe he's on to something.

Sabbath is God's antidote to the busyness and the mindless diversions of our culture. If we want to be formed into a people who don't look like that guy in the gym with an overdeveloped upper body and no foundation, if we don't want to settle for a mindless diversion instead of true rest, then we must recover the practice of taking Sabbath.

Sabbath is commanded in the Torah and sanctioned by Christ in the New Testament:

> "Remember the Sabbath day by keeping it holy. Six days you shall labor and do all your work, but the seventh day is a Sabbath to the LORD your God. On it you shall not do any work." (Exodus 20:8-10a)

> "Observe the Sabbath day by keeping it holy, as the LORD your God has commanded you. Six days you shall labor and do all your work, but the seventh day is a Sabbath to the LORD your God. On it you shall not

do any work . . . Remember that you were slaves in Egypt and that the LORD your God brought you out of there with a mighty hand and an outstretched arm. Therefore the LORD your God has commanded you to observe the Sabbath day." (Deuteronomy 5:12-15)

One Sabbath Jesus was going through the grainfields, and as his disciples walked along, they began to pick some heads of grain. The Pharisees said to him, "Look, why are they doing what is unlawful on the Sabbath?" . . . Then he said to them, "The Sabbath was made for man, not man for the Sabbath." (Mark 2:23-24, 27)

God tells his people there are certain ways he wants them to organize their time. The foundational element of God's plan was to work for six days, then to observe Sabbath. In fact, the practice originated with God's own observance of Sabbath.

God saw all that he had made, and it was very good. And there was evening, and there was morning—the sixth day. Thus the heavens and the earth were completed in all their vast array. By the seventh day God had finished the work he had been doing; so on the seventh day he rested from all his work. And God blessed the seventh day and made it holy, because on it he rested from all the work of creating that he had done. This is the account of the heavens and the earth when they were created. (Genesis 1:31-2:4)

God blessed the seventh day and made it *holy*. The mention of the word holy is incredibly important. This is the first time in the Scriptures that God ever designated something as holy. It wasn't a mountain or a shrine, an altar or a person. It wasn't a place or an idea. It was an *occasion*.

Sabbath is meant to be our physical and emotional recognition that we are not slaves. We are supposed to be free.

Time As a Commodity, Enemy, or Gift

Time has become either a commodity we try to save or an enemy we fight against. We love to *save* time. We talk about *spending* time or *investing* our time in someone or something. We say, "I'm running out of time." We will go to great lengths to gain back time. For example, for years the best-selling shampoo in America rose to the top not because it was a particularly effective product, but because it combined shampoo and conditioner in one step. It saved time. For years the leading pizza maker in the country became number one not because the pizza was good, but because the company promised delivery in thirty minutes or your pizza was free. They didn't sell pizza: they sold delivery time.

Time is also treated like an enemy. Plastic surgery is meant to reverse the effects of time on the body. Contemporary fashion trends have adults dressing more and more like young people. One of the hot retail clothing stores is called Forever 21. Americans spend somewhere around 1.5 to 2 billion dollars a year on anti-aging products. Lord, have mercy.

Time isn't meant to be a commodity that is optimized, invested, and stored. Time is not an enemy we are meant to fight against. Time is meant to be enjoyed. Time is a gift, a pleasurable part of God's good creation. Time can be a holy thing that shapes us into a holy people. Time is part of how we encounter the divine presence of God.

Enter the Sabbath. The very first Sabbath was observed by God. "God saw all that he had made; it was good, so very good" (see Genesis 1:31). Sabbath was actually God's recognition that all God had done on the first six days of creation was good. God had no regrets. There was no need to continue creating. God said, "Enough is enough. It's all good."

You've probably heard of the old painter who was arrested in an art museum for trying to keep working on one of his masterpieces that was on display there. For the artist, his work on his masterpiece was never finished. Sabbath is the opposite of that. God's first Sabbath was God's recognition that there was no reason to go on working forever.

The Sabbath will shape us because everything we do shapes us. We will either be shaped in illegitimate ways through constant busyness or we will observe Sabbath in a radical way and recover a proper relationship to time.

The Sabbath is holy.

The Sabbath is making all of time holy again.

The Sabbath can make us holy as well.

No More Restlessness

Most of us probably think that we work for six days, and then we rest on the Sabbath so that we have the energy to go back to work, as though the point of Sabbath is to help us to have the energy to deal with our real life. The Jewish concept of Sabbath is the inverse of that. You work six days to prepare for this one day when the world will be as it should be all the time. Sabbath is the day of the week when God's people and God's creation begin to look like they were created to be.

Theologian Walter Brueggemann often says that Americans are confused about Sabbath because we think it has to do with ceasing our work. He says that Sabbath is not the cessation of work but the cessation of restlessness. On the very first Sabbath day, God rested because God was content with what had been done. Sabbath was God's way of saying, "Enough!"[1] Perhaps we have lost the Sabbath because we have lost the ability to say "enough" in our society. If we lose the ability to say "enough," then we are doomed to a life of restlessness.

"Come unto me you who are weary and I will give you rest." Sabbath rest is a blessing, not an obligation. By declaring the Sabbath as holy, God is asking us to stop our perpetual motion and participate in God's holy time. We look at the blessings of our lives, we stare into the faces of our children, we laugh, we play, we take long walks, we take naps, we eat meals, we listen to the wind, we listen to the beating of our own heart, and we simply receive the day—that is Sabbath. Sabbath is the day when we delight in creation, when we delight in the moment—because the moment is holy.

Observing God's holy time can actually begin to make all of time holy again. Sabbath means we stop taking time for granted. It means we stop chasing our tails, looking for more, and regretting the past. Sabbath is our recognition that we are not generating our lives, but we are receiving them.

Sabbath shapes us into a peculiar kind of people.

And the world will notice.

Practical Sabbath

So, how should we observe Sabbath?

There is no magic formula, and nothing should be slavishly observed, nor should it become a dead burden. But here are some practical suggestions that might help.

First, use Saturday to prepare for Sabbath. Get all the chores done. Do the homework, clean the garage, mow the lawn, cook the food, and do the laundry. Get all the work out of the way on Saturday so that when Sunday comes, you can just breathe deeply and enjoy the passing of time.

Second, do Sabbath on Sunday, not another day of the week. It's become popular for pastors and others to say, "I take my Sabbath on Saturday." While there are certainly Christians who disagree with me, I believe that we cannot make that decision on our own. Since around the second century, Christians have celebrated Sabbath on Sunday. Early Christians kept the Jewish Sabbath on Saturday then had a resurrection celebration and love feast on Sunday. Over the years the church combined the two into one practice. Christians have been celebrating this way for around 1700 years. Sunday is our Sabbath. Often my family will observe Sabbath from sundown Saturday until sundown Sunday. It helps us to kick off Sabbath with a family meal and some fun time together.

Third, do Sabbath together. Sabbath is a corporate discipline. It starts with the family, extends to the church family, then to the neighbors, friends, and out into culture. Sabbath creates a ripple effect, but it starts with our decision to observe it together. Sabbath means long meals with friends, lingering after you eat for as long as you can. Sabbath is a corporate discipline. Get together, talk about life, delight in each other's presence and the presence of God.

Fourth, observe Sabbath as freedom, not slavery. Sabbath cannot be legalistic. It's a celebration of "enough," not a new religious dogma. We are children of the king! We are free! Order off the menu, people! What do you want to do?

- Drink your coffee and read the paper
- Play outside
- Go to a museum
- Watch a movie
- Listen to music
- Play live music
- Play board games
- Eat a meal with friends
- Have a long conversation
- Take a nap
- Watch football, golf, or Nascar
- Take a nap while watching football, golf, or Nascar
- Paint a picture
- Write a song
- Write in a journal
- Read the Scriptures

If you love to work in the garden, that's a great Sabbath exercise. If you love to cook, go for it. If you love to mow the lawn, then do it. Whatever brings you life, whatever ushers you into the presence of God, whatever you can do with others for no other reason than to delight in the goodness of time—that's a Sabbath activity.

Finally, protect the Sabbath. This is where it can get a little dicey. Our culture will try to push back on your taking Sabbath. Our kids don't play sports if it conflicts with our Sunday morning gathering with our community of faith. If it's a practice or a game on Sunday afternoon that will be fun for all of us, that's great. But if they don't want to go, we don't make them. On Sunday we do only what we want. When the culture wants a piece of Sabbath, we tell them "no."

Sabbath Speaks

Sabbath is integrally connected to mission. Mission is about going out into the world as salt and light. Mission is about organizing our lives in such a way that we image God to all creation. Sabbath is about organizing our time to make space for the sacred presence of the divine and each other.

Sabbath will change us. Sabbath will redeem our relationship to time and help us to connect with the divine. We will be transformed by the experience of Sabbath. Then we will be sent out into the culture having been transformed by the presence of God.

Taking Sabbath is a bold countercultural movement. When we observe Sabbath, it speaks to the culture around us, not in a judgmental way, but in a wise and loving way. It says, *You are missing the magic of time and God's creation. It's all around you, but you can't see it because you are too busy. You are trying to save time. You are fighting it like it's your enemy. You can go on chasing your tail, grasping for more, working on Saturday,* working on Sunday, working, working, working . . . But not us! We're just going to sit here, put our feet up, let our hair down, and drink in the presence of God, the joy of time, the miracle of being alive, the love of friends and neighbors, the taste of good food, the feeling of a lazy nap, the delight of every single moment!

Come rejoice with us.

Come learn how to enjoy time.

DISCUSSION QUESTIONS

When you were a child, how did your family observe Sabbath?

What does your calendar say about your life?

How have you treated time like a commodity? Like an enemy?

If you could have one day where you did anything, what would it be? Design a Sabbath practice and do it next Sunday.

Chapter 4

EUCHARISTIC LIFE:
BECOMING THE BODY OF CHRIST

Most of us are willing to accept the benefits of the body and blood of Christ. But few of us, I think, are willing, really willing, to go all the way in allowing that to make demands upon us. There's a sense in which if we want to share in his resurrection, we have to share in his death, you know?

When we do communion the prayer we pray every week is "Lord, bless this bread and this cup. May it be to us a spiritual food and drink. A means of your grace" (which is a John Wesley phrase, I think: "a means of your grace"). "And as we receive it into our bodies, may we receive you once again. Come live inside us. Make us new from the inside out. Then send us out into the world and let the world feast on us." I think there's a sense in which this life we have—this common life we have—is a life in which we share in the table of our Lord. This is both a benefit to us and makes huge demands upon our life.

In my church, when we do communion, the way we do it is everybody comes forward and we have a plate of bread and a cup. You take a piece of bread and dip it in the cup. It's called intinction. Nearly every week as I'm serving communion, a big part of my church comes to me and we say, "Remember the body and blood of Christ," and they say, "I will."

Our church has a lot of guys and girls who are homeless that come there. Most of these folks are still living on the street or out in the woods because they can't come in to the shelters because they're still using. So there's a lot of drug abuse and alcohol abuse still active there. We're just trying to be a place that they can come and encounter people who will just love them in the midst of what is maybe a pretty dark time for them.

So they come. They come forward to receive communion. One day I was serving communion and one of the guys came and some of the drugs that they use leave this black residue. Their fingernails turn really dark. Sometimes they haven't had a chance to shower in days. So he comes forward and takes the bread and dips it in the cup and his fingers go down into the cup a couple of inches. These black fingernails, just dirty hands. So I'm watching this happen and he receives it, which is always just a beautiful moment for me. Then out of the corner of my eye, I see the girl in line who's next—this young lady from our church, really neat girl. She saw what I saw, which was these fingernails go down into the cup. It was just this instant knowing she's next. She grabs a piece of bread and has to dip this in the cup and who knows, you know, what was on those fingernails? So she has to take this and receive it. I could just see her almost having to gag down the body of Christ. That moment sort of seared in my memory. This woman gagging down the body of Christ. I was thinking, there are times when if it doesn't seem like that, we have no idea what we're doing.

I'm reminded of the story where James's and John's mom comes to Jesus and says, "I want my kids to sit at your right and left." He says, "You don't know what you're asking." He says, "Can you share the cup I'm about to drink?" I think now I have a picture for part of what he meant. Those fingers dipping in there and then a "normal" white suburban person having to go next.

We come to the table every week not as this private religious exercise. It is a public exercise. This happens in kind of public space. Anybody can come witness this. So we share in kind of this Eucharistic life so that we can be made like Jesus and be sent out into the world and allow the world to feast on us.

COMMENTARY

At Redemption Church in Kansas City, where I serve as pastor, communion is the center of our worship. It's the climax. Everything we do before leads up to it: everything after is a way of living out what has happened there. We take the call to the table very seriously.

For years I was the worship leader at Redemption. I spent most Sunday mornings standing behind a guitar, leading the music, which means that I hardly ever served communion. When I began teaching every week, I also began serving communion. Redemption receives communion by serving in stages. The pastor serves the servers. The servers serve the congrega-tion. The congregation comes forward one by one to receive the feast. As each person comes forward, he or she takes a piece of bread, dips it in the cup, and the server says, "Remember the body and blood of Christ." Each person says back, "I will remember."

The first few weeks I served communion to people were almost too much for me to bear. I could hardly get through it without bursting into tears. I would look people in the eye as they came forward, calling them by name. Then I would hear myself say, "Remember the body and blood of Christ." Then another person would come and I would say it again: "Remember the body and blood of Christ." Over and over I heard myself saying it: "Remember the body and blood . . . body and blood . . . body and blood." As lines and lines of people came to receive communion, I found myself choking back tears, trying to control my emotions. I took deep breaths and tried not to make a scene.

The tears came anyway.

There was nothing I could do about it.

It was just so much body.

It was just so much blood.

The more I repeated those words, the more my heart connected with the reality that this isn't just some emblematic ritual. The death of Christ isn't some mythical *mojo* we apply to our lives like a magic elixir. I fought the urge to stop the whole thing and just say, "Do we realize what we are doing? Do we realize what has happened? We have tasted the body. We have tasted the blood."

It was too much.

Christ gave his body, his whole self, all that he was—to save and redeem all that we are.

I am undone by this.

The Body of Christ

The church is the body of Christ.

This is one of apostle Paul's favorite metaphors for the church. He wrote about it all the time.

> Just as each of us has one body with many members, and these members do not all have the same function, so in Christ we who are many form one body, and each member belongs to all the others. (Romans 12:4-5)

The church is connected together like the parts of a human body.

> And God placed all things under his feet and appointed him to be head over everything for the church, which is his body, the fullness of him who fills everything in every way. (Ephesians 1:22-23)

Paul says that the church is the "fullness of Christ." There is nothing of Jesus that is lacking in the church. We are the fullness of Christ, who is our head.

Let the peace of Christ rule in your hearts, since as members of one body you were called to peace. And be thankful. (Colossians 3:15)

The body is to be at peace, relating rightly to one another in unity and peace. This is what we're called to.

But in fact God has arranged the parts in the body, every one of them, just as he wanted them to be. If they were all one part, where would the body be? As it is, there are many parts, but one body. (1 Corinthians 12:18-20)

Somehow being the body of Christ is a corporate exercise that completes our personal identity. The body needs more than one member in order to image Jesus to the world.

Paul also connected the idea of the church as the body of Christ to the practice of receiving the Lord's Supper. He wrote:

Is not the cup of thanksgiving for which we give thanks a participation in the blood of Christ? And is not the bread that we break a participation in the body of Christ? Because there is one loaf, we, who are many, are one body, for we all partake of the one loaf. (1 Corinthians 10:16-17)

Somehow our participation in the Lord's Supper is part of how we all come to participate in the body of Christ. Because we share this feast, we share in a common life that is defined by Jesus Christ.

After the ascension the church became the way Christ would be physically present to the world. *We* are the body of Christ. *We* are the hands and feet of Jesus. *We* are the means by which Christ is present to the world. And, what the world needs more than anything is the presence of Christ.

As the church we embody God's intentions for the world in the way that we live our lives. Because we are committed to organizing our common life together in such a way that we image God, Jesus reaches up from inside us and writes his name all over our faces. Miraculously, as we live together within the life of the church, we become "his body, the fullness of him" (Ephesians 1:23). We become the way Jesus is present to the world.

This is not just a privilege: this is a calling, and it comes at a high cost.

Cruciform Life

When Jesus began to ask people to be his followers, he was honest with them about the fact that it was going to be hard. Jesus's call was not to pray a prayer to accept him as personal Lord and Savior. When you step back and take in the whole sweep of Jesus's message and his invitation to discipleship, it's fairly sobering. His call was not to believe certain facts or doctrines or to adopt a form of religious piety. His call was not to escape the world into a religious apathy, but to live a certain way of life. It was a new way of being a human being.

In the Gospel of Mark, Jesus appeared in the wilderness with John the Baptist. He came confessing the sins of his people, and his very first call was to "repent and believe." "Repent" is a tough word for us. Often we think it means to feel bad about our sins and ask for forgiveness, and that is certainly part of it, but there's more. To repent means we wake up and make a course correction. It means we stop pursuing our agenda for how the kingdom comes, and believe Jesus for his way. The Greek word is *metanoia*. The opposite of *metanoia* is *paranoia*. Paranoia is returning over and over to the same delusion. Repentance means that we leave our familiar delusions behind and trust Jesus completely for the new direction of our lives.

For those who would repent and believe, Jesus made another call: "Come and follow." That's the call of the disciple. His final call is where it gets really challenging. Jesus's most characteristic call in the Scriptures is to "take up your cross and follow me." It's a sobering progression:

> *Repent and believe.*
> *Come and follow.*
> *Go and die.*

Paul struggled to make sense of this calling on his own life. He wrote to the church at Philippi to try to explain the demand that Jesus was making on their lives. He said:

> Let the same mind be in you that was in Christ Jesus, who, though he was in the form of God, did not regard equality with God as something to be exploited, but emptied himself, taking the form of a slave, being born in human likeness. And being found in human form, he humbled himself and became obedient to the point of death—even death on a cross. Therefore God also highly exalted him and gave him the name that is above every name, so that at the name of Jesus every knee should bend, in heaven and on earth and under the earth, and every tongue should confess that Jesus Christ is Lord, to the glory of God the Father. (Philippians 2:5-11, *NRSV*)

There are three key words in this passage I want to tease out a little bit: *mind, exploited,* and *emptied.*

Mind: The word translated as "mind" is the Greek word *phroneo.* It doesn't mean "way of thinking": it involves a holistic pattern of thinking, feeling, and acting. The mind of Christ involves the whole person. Having the same mind is not just a mental or intellectual thing, but having the same pattern of thinking, feeling, and acting that Jesus had.

Exploited: The word translated "exploited" is the Greek word *harpagmos.* It means using for selfish gain. It means grasping after something in order to use it for your own self-enhancement. Jesus did not exploit the fact that he was one with the Father.

Emptied: The word translated "emptied" is the Greek word *kenosis.* It means humbling, emptying, pouring out until it's all gone. *Kenosis* is one of the key words for Paul's understanding of what it means to follow Jesus. Jesus self-emptied and we are to do the same.

Theologian Michael Gorman says that in this passage, the apostle Paul actually sets up a pattern that all disciples are meant to follow. The pattern is based on Jesus's way of life, and it serves as a model for how we are supposed to live. The pattern goes like this.

Although [x] – Status

Not [y] – Exploiting

But [z] – Self-emptying

Although [x]: Jesus was in the form of God. Not [y]: He did not exploit his equality with God. But [z]: Jesus emptied himself and became as a slave.

This is the pattern of Jesus's life. This is also meant to be the pattern of our lives.[1]

If we want to have the "mind" of Christ, this is how we do it. We follow the pattern set out for us in the life of Jesus. Paul seemed to believe that Jesus was not just teaching us how to live, but he was actually revealing the nature of God. We follow this pattern not just because Jesus said to. We follow it because this is who God is. *The God revealed in Jesus is the self-emptying God.*

So when we talk about having the mind of Christ—the same pattern of thinking, feeling, and acting—this is the pattern. Although we have some status, we do not exploit it, but empty ourselves and become like a slave.

But that's not where it ends. The second half of the pattern from Philippians 2 is that God highly exalted Jesus and gave him the name that is above every other name. Everyone will confess his lordship some day. The first half of the pattern is a humbling and emptying. The second half is where we are lifted up again—only we are lifted not by our own efforts or abilities, but by the power of God.

Both James and Peter mention this same pattern: "Humble yourselves before the Lord, and he will lift you up" (James 4:10). "Humble yourselves, therefore, under God's mighty hand, that he may lift you up in due time" (1 Peter 5:6). Our part is humbling and self-emptying. God's part is lifting us up in due time. So, what status do you enjoy? Are you:

- rich
- powerful
- of high social standing

- a parent
- a boss
- smart
- great at relationships
- beautiful
- successful
- strong

These are just a few examples of status. If you were to take some time to think it through, you could come up with a long list of your own. The Jesus way of life teaches us that we are not meant to exploit that status for personal gain, but that we must empty ourselves of that status on behalf of the world.

Jesus's entire life was spent emptying himself of status. It is the central theme of his famous teaching from Luke 17: "'Whoever tries to keep his life will lose it, and whoever loses his life will preserve it'" (verse 33). Michael Gorman describes this as "the cruciform life." Our lives, as followers of Jesus, are supposed to take on the form and shape of the cross. When we imitate Jesus, we imitate Jesus on the cross, laying down his life for the sake of the world. That's the cruciform life.[2]

Here's the thing. It's easy to receive the benefits of the body of Christ. But it's hard to deal with the demands it makes upon our lives. It is no small thing to empty ourselves daily of the status we enjoy. It goes against our culture and our instincts to always choose the humble road.

Discipleship will challenge us to the core. It requires constant willingness to die to ourselves and to others. Paul knew it was difficult, and he labored to convince people it would be worth it. He wrote, "Therefore, I urge you, brothers, in view of God's mercy, to offer your bodies as living sacrifices, holy and pleasing to God" (Romans 12:1). We worship Jesus with a holistic pattern of thinking, feeling, and acting. When we worship Jesus, we worship him not only with our lips, but with our lives. This is the cruciform life of discipleship.

Eat My Flesh. Drink My Blood.

There is no more challenging teaching in the Scriptures than Jesus's call to the cruciform life. The call to lay down our life, to become a living sacrifice, to take up our cross, these are the things we enact and embody every time we receive communion or the Eucharist.

Early on in the life of the church, communion, or the Lord's Supper, became known as the Eucharist. This term actually comes from the Greek word *eucharistia*, which means "giving thanks." The earliest use of *Eucharist* in connection with the Lord's Supper comes from 1 Corinthians 11:24 when Paul describes how the first Eucharist was celebrated. Paul says that Jesus broke the bread and gave thanks (*eucharistesas*). The Lord's table is the center of the Eucharistic life—a life that gives thanks.

In John chapter six, Jesus introduced the concept of the Eucharistic life to his followers. He said, "'Those who eat my flesh and drink my blood have eternal life'" (John 6:54, *NRSV*). Can you imagine hearing that for the first time? Hebrews didn't drink blood: that's what the pagans did. It sounds as bizarre today as it did back then. After Jesus said it, a bunch of his followers left. It was too much for them and they bailed. We don't know how many left, but from the way the Scriptures tell the story, it seems to have really bothered Jesus. He turned to the twelve and said, almost sarcastically, "'Do you also wish to go away?'" (John 6:67, *NRSV*).

It was a fair question. The cruciform life that Jesus was proposing made absolutely no sense to begin with, but the insistence that they must eat his body and drink his blood? This was pretty out there. Peter seems to have spoken for the whole group. He simply said, "'Lord, to whom can we go? You have the words of eternal life'" (John 6:68, *NRSV*).

Where else can we go? Who else has the words of life? I love this passage because I really don't want to live a cruciform life. I don't want to die to myself. I like to enjoy my status. I want to use my status to make my own life better. But like Peter and the others, I have become convinced that this Jesus is the Holy One of God. Only he has the words of life.

Where else can I go? He's the only way.

If we want to truly live, we must live as Jesus lived.

If we want eternal life, we must die as Jesus died.

The self-emptying God came into the world as a self-emptying man. The world's true Lord, the ruler of all creation, poured his life out to make a way back to God. And so God will put people back together this way— through cruciform lives. And God will put the world back together this way—through a cruciform church.

The pattern of thinking, feeling, and acting we are meant to imitate is the one Jesus lived. All of us who are a part of the body of Christ, we assume this cruciform posture. We become part of the bloody body of Jesus, sacrificing itself for the life of the world. It's a beautiful thing. But don't ever think it's easy. It's not. Many of us are willing to receive the benefits of Christ's body. Few of us are willing to receive his cross as well.

At my church when we receive our communion by stages, the pastor serves the servers, the servers serve the congregation, and then there is one final movement. The congregation serves the world. We go out into the world as salt and light, and we let the world feast on us.

The world consumes us.

The mission of God consumes us.

We become the body of Christ.

As we become like him in his death, we also get to share in his resurrection.

DISCUSSION QUESTIONS

Make a list of all of the ways in which you hold status, from big to small, significant to insignificant. What would it look like for you to empty yourselves of the status you enjoy?

To empty ourselves of status instead of exploiting it goes against the grain of our culture. How might this result in actual suffering?

Sometimes when we die to ourselves and others, we get a glimpse of resurrection: in some small way, there is a payoff. How have you seen this in your life?

Have you ever died to someone, or something, and then witnessed new life grow from that experience?

Chapter 5

LANGUAGING GOD:
THE GIFT OF PUBLIC SPEECH

I feel like too often the way we use language—we use it in dualistic ways. But oftentimes language becomes a way that we chop the world up in illegitimate ways. So what happens is we meet the world and we meet up with a person, or a place, or a thing, or an idea, and immediately we stack it in one of two categories: *things I like* or *things I don't like*. Or, *things that are like me, things that are unlike me*. So we'll create these two piles. A pile of good stuff, which of course we think is all the stuff we subscribe to. Then there's this other stuff over here that we then demonize and call the negative and try to eliminate. We want to blow it up. Jesus had this crazy way of undermining that whole deal.

Any way you could chop up the world in first century Palestine—Jews and Greeks, men and women, clean and unclean—he would go buddy up with the "wrong" side. He would touch them. He would eat with them. He would befriend them. So you start to get a sense, especially over the wide sweep of the Gospels, that perfection for Jesus was not the division and then elimination of the negative. He lives his life like this [opens his hands wide], not like this [closes his hands]. With this "yes." Perfection for Jesus was not the elimination of the negative. It's the redemption of it. Somehow resurrecting it. Bringing new life to it. He's about redemption.

One of the things we need to do in the church is learn how to use language as a way to accept people, first as bearers of the image of God, as God's precious children, so that we can help them to join the path of redemption.

I just read a book this summer—Tina Fey's book, *Bossypants*. She talks about the nature of improv. I'm not an actor, so improv, like charades, just sounds like a horrible deal to me. She said, in improv, the first rule of improv is, you must say "yes." So if somebody comes in an improv scene and says, "I'm a dog," if you say "no," scene's over: there is no improv. So what you say is "yes." Not just "yes," but you say "yes, and." So what they say is, "I'm a dog," and you say, "Yes, and you're a dog who likes opera." And they say, "Yes, I'm a dog who likes opera," and this is how improv goes.

If you say "no," there's no conversation, instantly no conversation, no improvisation. What the Christian says is, "yes, and," which is very different from, "yes, but," which is what we often want to say—"yes, but"—and then we offload whatever doctrinal thing we're trying to get people to capitulate to. The nature of the "yes" is you're saying "yes" to the person. It's not an indiscriminate "yes" like, "yes, everything you believe is right and perfect." It's just a "yes, you." Like, "yes, I see you. I recognize the divine spark in you and I say 'yes' to that, and resurrection." *And*, not *but*. Not "yes, but I'm going to need you to believe these things: otherwise I can't accept you." It's "yes, and let me tell you about this hope I have and this way I've been taught to see the world that I think can make you human like human was meant to be." Always from the very beginning.

I think that's actually a pretty decent image for how we use language in a church. We don't just say "yes, indiscriminately yes to anything." We say "yes, and." Then we talk about what redemption looks like and what resurrection looks like. So where the rest of the world says "despair," we say "resurrection." Where the rest of the world says "hopeless," we say "hopeful." We use a completely different set of words and language that describe a completely different vision of reality, and as we do this, it's like God just appears and happens in the moment and leaves us forever changed. Language is powerful. It can do this.

COMMENTARY

When Galileo began to really perfect his telescope, he became the first to peek outside our normal view of reality. As the story goes, the night Galileo first saw the moons of Jupiter he went home and wrote, "I render infinite thanks to God for being so kind to make me alone the first observer of marvels kept hidden in obscurity for all bygone ages."[1]

It doesn't seem as though it ever occurred to Galileo, at least early on, that his work was a threat to the Christian faith. It was a deeply spiritual thing to him to learn new things and grow in his understanding of the natural world. His spontaneous response was to honor God. But, he famously came into conflict with the Catholic Church over his belief that the earth revolved around the sun, and he was later placed under house arrest until he died.

One of the most interesting details of the story is that many of the scientists who opposed Galileo refused to ever look through the telescope. They literally closed their eyes and refused to see what he had seen. You would think they would at least want to take a look out of sheer curiosity before they passed judgment. Why would they refuse to see?

It's a natural human response to be skeptical of new ideas. Yet it is possible that there is an even deeper phenomenon at work. Father Richard Rohr calls this phenomenon "dividing the field." Simply put, dividing the field is what we do when we meet any reality. We encounter a person, an idea, an event, and we immediately judge it. We divide reality into one of two groups:

1. Things I like that are like me.

2. Things I don't like that are not like me.

Humans do this constantly. However you wish to divide God's good creation into parts, you can do it: male/female, black/white, rich/poor, educated/uneducated, attractive/unattractive, Republican/Democrat, northerner/southerner, and on and on. Typically, we divide the field; then we show preference to one side and disdain for the other.

Jesus never did this. Jesus ate with tax collectors, defended prostitutes, conversed openly with women, touched lepers, touched the unclean, helped Gentiles, made Samaritans into heroes of his stories, and generally made friends with all the wrong people. However you could divide the field in the ancient world, Jesus would intervene on behalf of the wrong side.

Jesus went out of his way to avoid eliminating anybody. Jesus didn't seem at all interested in destroying the problematic. Perfection for Jesus was not the elimination of the negative side of reality, but the redemption of it. As it turns out, Jesus will stop at nothing to make sure that everything and everyone gets a shot at the kingdom of God.

Where God Happens

Rowan Williams is the head of the Church of England, and a wise man. A few years back he wrote a book called *Where God Happens*, in which he taught that one of the most important aspects of what it means to be a Christian is that every encounter we have with people, places, things, and ideas is an opportunity for God to "happen" to us and to them. The Christian's most sacred vocation when relating to another human being is to try to become the conduit through which that person comes into contact with the risen Savior. As we relate to one another, God can "happen" to us over and over.

Williams points out that it's no big deal to believe that my spiritual life will shape the way I relate to my neighbor. The trick is to believe that the way I relate to my neighbor will have a significant effect on my spiritual life. Williams says, "Everything begins with this vision and hope: to put the neighbor in touch with God in Christ."[2]

It's a strange thing to think about—that God can "happen" to somebody. That thought almost feels sacrilegious. Sometimes when God happens to us, it is this full body experience of the divine that our intellect can't touch, our words can't explain, and our emotions can't contain. Sometimes it is more subdued, just a sixth sense that something transcendent is going on, like our hearts are strangely warmed.

Over and over in the Scriptures, we see God bursting onto the scene with the promise of new life through the power of God's presence in Christ. Through him, God is on the loose and willing to relate personally to every human life.

It feels odd to make this claim. Shouldn't the creator and sustainer of the universe be out there solving world hunger or fighting the devil? Doesn't God have better things to do? Not if you believe in resurrection. At the center of the incarnation of Jesus Christ—at the center of his teachings, death, and resurrection—we find a very simple promise: God can happen to anyone, anytime, anyplace, and we get to be a part of that.

Here's the thing. If we spend all of our lives dividing the field and counting people out, then God cannot happen to us and to those with whom we are in contact. Slicing up the world into things we like that are like us and things we don't like that are not like us then trying to destroy the other side will quell the activity of God. If we divide the field, God will not happen.

Paying Attention

When we spend our lives in a "dividing the field" posture, we foster inattention in our own lives. When we do this, we miss out on the chance to see God happen.

I have several friends who are homeless. For the most part they are homeless because they have serious problems—emotional problems, active addictions, mental illness—that have resulted in a pretty heartbreaking reality. I used to do my best to ignore the homeless. I'd see them on the street and try not to make eye contact. Now that I know some of them personally, I know their names and their stories: now that I care about them and feel like they care about me as well, I can't ignore them anymore.

We don't generally treat homeless people with open hostility. It's not often that somebody yells, "Get a job, you lazy bum." We don't do that because it would be cruel. What we do is treat them with indifference. We ignore them. We make them invisible. That's inattention. Inattention is a major problem for the Christian. Inattention speaks—it says things. It tells people they don't matter. When we meet the world with indifferent inattention, we reject our God-given assignment to usher others into contact with the God who has moved heaven and earth to save them.

A couple of years ago my car died and we bought a Volkswagen to replace it. I had been driving my VW for at least six months when a friend taught me to watch oncoming cars as they pass by me. She said that if you pay attention, you can often see someone yell, "slug bug" and smack the person next to them in the car. This, as it turns out, is great fun. I had forgotten all about the "slug bug" game and honestly never thought to look for it. I had been missing this entertaining phenomenon for months. Now that I know to watch for it, I see it happen all the time. Now I'm paying attention.

Ever buy a car that is new to you, a make or model that you never really paid any attention to? Before you bought the car you never noticed these things on the road. After buying one yourself, it's as though all of the sudden you see them everywhere you go. That's the power of paying attention.

Paying attention to people speaks volumes. "Seeing" someone is a kind of language. Refusing to make people invisible is the first step to letting God happen. Part of what it means to follow Jesus is that we learn how to pay attention to the world. We learn how to see. Instead of dividing the field, judging one side, and trying to ignore or destroy them, the Christian sees everything and everyone. The Christian has compassion for everything, the way Jesus did. Part of what it means to be a disciple is that we have to learn how to see again.

Having a few homeless friends that I can hang out with every week has had a profound impact on my life. Through their friendship I have learned how to see the homeless. If we truly knew how much we had in common with the beggar on the street, if we knew that we are all spiritual beggars, perhaps we could find a way to connect—to allow God to happen to us.

Healthy people find ways to stay connected to the needs of the world. Healthy churches do the same. This begins with the ability to see. When healthy people and healthy churches find ways to see the broken, to stand in solidarity with the marginalized, sin is destroyed. When we who have found forgiveness take that forgiveness to others, the power of sin is crushed. God happens. We become the place where God happens to them, to us, and to the world.

Silence Is a Language

Sometimes the first step toward learning how to see, or how to pay attention, is to find a place for silence in our lives. Silence is one of the world's most powerful teachers. Silence teaches us to pay attention to ourselves. In silence our normal patterns of thinking, feeling, and acting assault us. They scream, "Think me! Feel me! Get up and do something productive!" If we will outlast the voices in our head and push through to genuine silence, we will begin to learn from the silence. What the silence will teach you, I cannot say. It is a lesson meant only for you. It is a secret locked away in your heart, which will come out only through sustained periods of silence.

Silence teaches us to pay attention to God. God wants to speak. God is speaking all the time. The problem isn't that God never speaks; it is that we never listen. God loves nothing more than a bunch of people who will sit in silence and say, "Speak, Lord, for your servant is listening." When God sees us in silence, waiting for a word, that's when a word usually comes.

Silence teaches us to pay attention to the world around us. If we'll stop checking our phones and our e-mails, texting, tweeting, watching television, and begin to find a place for silence, we'll begin to see the world in a very different light. Silence is the place where the world will speak to those who listen. Silence is how we can begin to just be present to the world again. In silence, we can begin to hear the lives of those around us.

But we don't do silence.

Gordon Hempton is a sound engineer and naturalist who wrote a book called *One Square Inch of Silence*. He says that the possibility for silence in nature is being drowned out. Flight patterns for airplanes, highways, electrical lines, machines, and vehicles crisscross even some of the most remote parts of the United States. Silence is disappearing quickly.

Hempton wrote that in 1983, he could find twenty-one places in Washington State where he could record a fifteen-minute noise-free interval. Twenty years later, only three of them were left. The other eighteen were interrupted an average of every ninety seconds. Silence is hard to find, even in the wilderness. Hempton said it used to take just a few hours for him to make a recording of fifteen minutes of uninterrupted silence. Now it takes him over two hundred hours of recording.[3]

How will we find time for silence? How will we find a place for silence? We live in a culture that is never silent. If you want silence, you are going to have to work for it, chase it, create it, and protect it.

Fight, Flight, and Fidelity

Once we begin to pay attention instead of dividing the field, and once we've allowed silence to teach us to listen to ourselves, God, and the world around us, then we need to figure out how to talk to one another. Talking is harder than you think. Theologian Stanley Hauerwas is fond of saying that the only conviction many Christians have left is that they are convinced that Jesus was nice, so we ought to be nice as well.[4] While I don't think we need to be mean, we also don't want to allow our refusal to "divide the field" to make us wishy-washy. We can't allow our desire to be nice to cause us to cease to believe that Jesus is the world's true Lord.

I do a lot of writing. Sometimes when I write articles for the *Huffington Post* or on Paperback Theology (my blog), I'll get some people all riled up and they'll attack me for what I've said. If everyone involved is polite and generous, these exchanges can be really productive. Good theological disagreements can be powerful in terms of correcting my bad language or beliefs.

I once posted an article on my blog in which I used the word "heresy" to refer to a certain doctrine. I really shouldn't have used that word. I should have called it an erroneous belief or something milder. I was dividing the field and counting one side out. As the comments flowed in, I noticed that I was keeping tabs on who agreed with my side and who did not. Then a couple of true friends called me out for using the word "heresy." They said, "You are calling me a heretic." I realized I didn't want to count them out.

When we have a conflict with other people, a disagreement, or when we feel threatened or accused, often our reaction is to find someone who will agree with us. When I feel vulnerable I look for someone to reassure me that I'm wonderful and smart. This approach might mitigate the pain in the short run, but in the long run it is like drinking saltwater. Keeping the company of those who will affirm us is comfortable and safe, but it can also keep us from learning the truth about ourselves. We need to know how to experience conflict without self-justification being our only response. Conflict is the only thing that will ever help us to change and grow.

Once we realize that we disagree with someone, the trick is to live in deep disagreement without having to kill each other, run away, or draw people in on our side of the argument. We want to be nice, and we should be nice. But we really need to learn how to fight. By fight I don't mean destroy each other, or "win" an argument. We need to learn how to faithfully articulate deeply held convictions in the face of direct opposition. It is hard to do, but it is healthy.

When a significant disagreement gets going, some people will run away immediately. Running away is just a form of escapism. Flight is about denying ourselves and others the opportunity to grow. It is a powerful thing to deny ourselves the luxury of solving all of our problems by running away physically or emotionally. Flight ends the discussion before it starts. It breaks communion. Flight keeps us from taking responsibility for our own sins.

Christian maturity is integrally connected to the concept of *fidelity*. Fidelity means sticking around no matter what. Fidelity means refusing to meet the roadblocks and frustrations of our common life by moving on. Fidelity forces us to deal with our own unreality.

God's advice is nearly always to stay. To stick it out. When we allow God to move and change us through the tension, Christians learn how to disagree without feeling like we need to kill each other. Fidelity forces us to face the painful reality that all of our problems are not located conveniently outside of ourselves. You are not my problem. I am my problem. You are my brother or sister. My job is not to force you to think like me: my job is to try to put you in touch with God. Many times, the most powerful way this can happen is through fidelity.

As a pastor I've counseled many couples who are experiencing marital problems. Infidelity is the worst of all. The erosion of trust that comes from infidelity is devastating. However, as I've watched couples stick it out I've seen them come out on the other side with incredible marriages. When fidelity is practiced, especially in the midst of powerful tension and pain, the power of God is released in that situation. God happens to both parties.

We are going to fight—it will undoubtedly happen. But we have to reject flight as a means of solving conflict. We have to practice fidelity in the face of all disagreements. I have often told my congregation that our ability to participate in the kingdom of God does not depend upon having all the right answers to all the right questions. Our ability to participate in the kingdom depends upon our ability to stick together through the power of the Holy Spirit. Come hell or high water, if nobody leaves, we will slowly look more and more like Jesus.

Languaging God in Public Space

Okay, let's say you are with me so far. You are willing to refuse to divide the field and destroy the other side. You desire to embrace the call to try to put other people in touch with God. You have embraced the practice of silence in order to know how to better use language. You have chosen fidelity to God and to the church instead of self-justification or fleeing. Conflicts are not destroying you or those around you but are helping you to grow in your faith and in your relationship to the body.

How does living this way impact public space?

First and foremost, making these choices will impact public space because you will be a transformed person. Living in the way I just described will absolutely transform you from the inside out. You will react to others, to yourself, to God, to events, and ideas in a very different manner. If we will allow our life with the people of God to become permeated with fidelity to God and each other, we will quite simply be a new creation. There is no greater witness to the veracity of the gospel than a transformed life.

Apart from that, I have very little practical advice for how to language God in public space. If you are transformed by God's love and grace, if you are transformed by the word of God and the communion of the saints, it will just happen.

Transformed people tip their waitresses because they know their job isn't easy. Transformed people look the checkout person in the eye at the supermarket; they use moments like these as chances to connect with other human beings. Transformed people let people cut in line when they are in a hurry. Transformed people greet interruptions as opportunities rather than inconveniences.

Transformed people speak with confidence about how resurrection is breaking into their lives. Transformed people look like light. Transformed people taste like salt. Wherever they go, whatever they do, God happens in their midst.

DISCUSSION QUESTIONS

Have you ever seen God happen?

How do you divide the field?

How do you find silence?

Have you ever run away from an argument rather than finishing it?

How would our lives be different if we learned how to have conflict, fights, and disagreements without running away? What would this say to the world around us?

Chapter 6

CHRISTIAN POLITICAL LIFE

One of the weird parts about being a pastor is I feel like a big part of my job is to try to convince people that up is down. That there's this way the world is, and the way of the cross is just different. This is what is meant by "you'll find your life by losing it." If you try to find your life, you'll actually lose it. Up is down. That's a tough sell. Especially in a political situation where we actually have a little bit of power. Early Christians had no power. A lot of times now I think what we want to do is climb into the seat of power. That's Herod's chair, you know. That's Pilate's chair. And the one we imitate is Jesus, who stands before them and actually says very little, and is a little cagey and a little slipper with how he interacts with power.

So part of what it means to be a disciple is whatever the pecking order is in the world is reversed for us. So what we care about is the least of these. We say things like, "The job of government is not to make sure what's mine is mine. The job of government is to kind of restrain evil and do as little harm as possible."

The root word for liberal is liberate. There are some people who are liberators. The root of conservative is conserve. There are some people whose heart is just a conserver thing. I think it's funny that if I ask you, "Are you a yes person or a no person?" and I don't give you any more information, you know the answer to that. Are you a yes person or a no person? I'm a no person. When my kids say, "Can I go outside and play?" I say, "No!" And then I get to thinking, well, is there a good reason you can't? Then I say yes. My wife is a yes person: she says yes.

It can be dangerous, especially raising kids, if both parents are yes people. You can grow up with wild children with no self-discipline. They're both no people? You'll grow up with these cautious kids who are afraid to take risks. Oftentimes, yes people are attracted to no people. I think there's a reason for this because we need conservers—no people. We need liberators— yes people. We need them in the same place, not defined by their yes or their no. But defined by gospel. So our fidelity is not to a bent. Our fidelity is to Jesus. Our goal is gospel.

I think we do politics primarily with our lives, not with our lips. So our job, I think, is not so much to run the world as it is to bear witness that Jesus is the world's true Lord. That is, if Jesus is Lord then Caesar is not. So the claim of Jesus's lordship has no limits. The foundation for the Christian is that we are first and foremost citizens of heaven. So I think one of the mistakes that we often make as Christians is we will buddy up with one political system or another. Or one economic system or another. Or we'll buddy up with a political party. Or one or the other. Then baptize it with enough religious language to make us feel okay about it. So our first identity is I'm a child of God. I'm a Christian. This is my identity.

I really believe that Christianity, Christian, is a political distinction which claims Jesus is Lord, and if Jesus is Lord, Caesar is not. It does not make sense in the rest of culture. I mean, it really is like saying up is down. The way to organize in a way that proclaims Christ is Lord is how do I sacrifice myself on behalf of the life of the world? And somehow Christ is going to take what we do, on behalf of the ordering of the chaos that, and this could even mean political discourse or be a part of city governments, or you know, whatever, how we organize our lives will somehow be drawn up into his redemptive project.

COMMENTARY

Theologian and ethicist Stanley Hauerwas is fond of saying that he represents the "Tonto Principle" in Christian ethics. He's referring to the old television program in which the Lone Ranger and his sidekick, Tonto, traveled around the Old West, fighting for truth and justice. Hauerwas says that one time the two were surrounded by twenty thousand Sioux in the Dakotas. The Lone Ranger turned to Tonto and said, "We're in a pretty bad fix. What do you think we ought to do?" Tonto looked at him and said, "What do you mean 'we,' white man?" Hauerwas believes this is the movement we all need to learn how to make—recovering the Christian "we" from the American "we."[1]

Christian identity is meant to be all consuming. Becoming part of the people of God redefines the way we relate to every other part of our lives, including our family, country, profession, and even the earth itself. The cross stands not only at the center of history, but at the center of every Christian's life.

This is part of what is signified by the act of baptism. In our baptism we renounce our citizenship in the kingdoms of this world and are joined together as citizens of the kingdom of God. Baptism is a profoundly political act. Race, family, gender, profession, political party, economic systems, country, union, guild—those things go down under the water and don't come back up. Only our identity as "Christian" comes through those waters.

The baptized person is a new reality constituted by God, through Jesus, in the power of the Holy Spirit. The old person dies. The old way of being dies. A new creation is alive and walking around. As the apostle Paul was fond of saying, we are "in Christ." Our identity is hidden with Christ in God. God becomes the one in whom we live and move and have our being.

Only after we embrace this all-consuming identity as children of God can we enter into other ways of belonging appropriately. Once we recover the Christian "we," we can discover what it means to belong to a race, family, spouse, gender, profession, political party, and so on in the light of our prior commitment to God. The first step is to surrender to our primary identity as the sons and daughters of God.

In Galatians 2:20, Paul wrote, "It is no longer I who live, but Christ who lives in me" (*ESV*). I think it is sometimes helpful to use that verse to think about how I relate to all of my other identities. So, I will say, "It is no longer *a man* who lives, but Christ who lives in me." Or, "It is no longer *a pastor* who lives, but Christ who lives in me." Or, "It is no longer *a husband* who lives, but Christ who lives in me." For years and years, the most difficult one for me to say was always, "It is no longer *an American* who lives, but Christ who lives in me." National identity runs deep.

Christianity As Advanced Citizenship

American citizenship makes many demands upon our lives that we rarely think about. Every eighteen-year-old male has to register for the draft. We pay taxes and register to vote. If we register to vote, then we are required to serve on jury duty. We have to buy a license from the government in order to get married, open a business, or catch a fish. Our children are asked to pledge allegiance to our flag in the classroom and at public events. We are taught to sing nationalistic hymns like "God Bless America," "America the Beautiful," "My Country 'Tis of Thee," and "The Star-Spangled Banner."

Most Christian Americans take part in these things without ever considering what we are doing in light of our baptism. For the most part we have conflated the Christian "we" with the American "we." Yet, I think there is a sense in which we all know that God's kingdom transcends nationality. We know that the Christian "we" is not the same as the American "we," but we have been so shaped by our participation in the American "we" that we don't know how to separate the two. For most Christians living in America, recovering the Christian "we" from the American "we" is major surgery.

Now, we also must say that Jesus and the United States are not mutually exclusive. Jesus and any country are not mutually exclusive, for that matter. Jesus is no respecter of nationality, race, gender, and so on. Right at this very moment, Christians are living, thriving, and imaging God in nearly every nation across the world, and Jesus is very happy about that. As Christians, then, we openly confess that it is a far greater blessing to be a citizen of the kingdom of God than to be a citizen of any country. To embrace Christian identity and let it go "all the way down" is one of the more advanced moves the Christian learns to make.

In a place like America, where political conversations are polarized and ugly, we all sense there is an inherent danger in involving ourselves in politics, especially when we begin the political discussion with a confession that our primary concern is not the advancement of a country, but the advancement of the kingdom of God. Participating in the organization of society is a sacred calling, part of our original vocation to have dominion, to fill the earth, subdue it, till it, keep it, and cause it to bear fruit. The call to organize our common life so we image God to all creation involves polity and organization.

To reconcile our citizenship in the kingdom of God with our national citizenship is advanced work. It is difficult. It will not happen without deep reflection and careful consideration. It will not happen without intentional discipleship to the way of the cross.

Rejecting the Categories

In the United States we have two major political parties. While I cannot even begin to describe their beliefs accurately, it is generally safe to say the Republican Party tends toward conservatism, and the Democratic Party tends toward liberalism. There are exceptions, of course, as neither party is monolithic. In the end the political, economic, and social agendas of each party are beside the point. What's most interesting to me is the underlying assumption that feeds all political parties in general. To understand this we need only pay attention to what each group promises.

Politicians and parties on both the right and the left operate upon the very same underlying assumption. They each believe that they should be running the world. Both parties believe that if they could run the world, things would be fine. The bedrock assumption common to both political parties is, "Vote for me and the utopia we all desire will finally happen."

The only problem with this assumption is that it isn't true.

Most of us can recognize the utopian promise as a lie. How many times must we vote one party or the other into office as they promise us change only to realize that our problems remain? Often, people who become disillusioned with the two major parties will attempt to create a third party, only to discover that it too is founded on the same failed assumption. All parties operate under the same underlying assumption. This is why all parties perennially over promise and under deliver. They do not possess the power to do what they promise to do. Their failed assumption is that they know how best to run the world.

Christians can readily confess that we do not know how best to run the world. The fundamental Christian assumption is that the problems we face are actually the result of our attempts to run the world ourselves. Apart from Christ, there is no perfect ruler. Apart from God's agenda, all other agendas fall short.

Jesus is the world's true Lord, and if Jesus is Lord, *we are not*. You see, the particular agenda of either American political party, whether it is conservative, liberal, or moderate, is not what causes the problem for the Christian. There are things about each party with which the Christian would agree and things about each party with which the Christian would disagree. The problem of party affiliation for the Christian lies in our confession that Jesus is Lord. If Jesus is Lord, the Republican way is not. If Jesus is Lord, the Democrat way is not.

Political agendas exist on a sort of continuum—liberals on the left, conservatives on the right, moderates in the middle, while Jesus Christ transcends them all. Jesus doesn't exist on that continuum. Jesus exists on a plane of his own. Once we've made the assumption that neither agenda is able to deliver on the promises they make, our allegiance can never be to a party agenda, but only to Jesus.

The claim that Jesus is the world's true Lord is not a fix-all declaration. In fact it can cause more problems than it solves. In our society the involvement of religion in politics has increasingly tended toward two diverging camps: *Fundamentalism* and *Secularism*.

Religious fundamentalism involves the impulse to institutionalize religious control over society. Fundamentalist beliefs are rooted in sacred texts like the Bible or the Koran, which they take to be above criticism. Fundamentalists become strident, rigid, and often shrill about the certainty that their way of running the world is the right way. Fundamentalism is defined in part by its all-out opposition to secularism.

Secularism holds that we have to keep God and religion out of public life, especially the political realm. Secularist beliefs are rooted in science and the natural world, which they take to be above criticism. Secularists become strident, rigid, and often shrill about the certainty that their way of running the world is the right way. Secularism is defined in part by its all-out opposition to fundamentalism.

Notice any similarities? When we explore and describe the phenomenon of religious fundamentalism and secularism, we find that each exists in roughly the same categories as the other. They define themselves in opposition to each other, and each operates under the assumption that if they could just destroy the opposition, they could run the world properly. In this manner they are not unlike political parties.

Here's the thing, though. Jesus transcends them all.

Jesus exists on a plane of his own. Like political parties, Jesus calls them all into question because they make a promise they cannot deliver.

Now, some people will simply claim that religious beliefs are meant to be personal and private. However, as we explored in the Introduction, Jesus's kingdom is not *from* this world, but it is most certainly *for* this world. God cares about every aspect of life, including the way we organize ourselves. Each Christian is called to live as though Jesus's lordship is not simply a matter of opinion but is an objective reality. Therefore, one cannot relegate faith to the private sphere because the public sphere belongs to God.

The most essential move that Christians must learn to make in terms of politics is to refuse to locate themselves along either continuum—be it conservative versus liberal, Republican versus Democrat, or secularism versus fundamentalism. We identify with Jesus and Jesus alone.

However, there is a downside. It doesn't *have* to be a downside, but I'm afraid most of us will see it as such. Here it is: *Identifying with Jesus will make us permanent outsiders.* There is no way to avoid this reality. We can only embrace it. We are resident aliens. This world is not our home because our citizenship is in the kingdom of heaven. Not only that, but our conviction is that the kingdom of God advances via the cruciformity modeled in the life of Jesus. You find your life by losing it. You lose your life by finding it.

Missional Politics

This is tough to imagine, I know. So, let's try a different kind of metaphor for how our faith and politics are supposed to work. Think about the way firefighters live and work. Several men in my congregation work for the fire department. I've learned that this group is like a fraternity, or a brotherhood, and they take their identity as firefighters very seriously. It's not just a job to them. It's a way of life. This is true, at least in part, because their job demands that they risk their lives to save someone else. Firefighters are defined by their mission.

Christians have a similar kind of vocational calling. Our identity as Christians doesn't just concern our religious beliefs. Our faith is like a fraternity, a brotherhood and sisterhood. Most of us take our identity as Christians very seriously. It's not just a belief system to us. It is a way of life. This is true, at least in part, because our faith demands that we lay down our lives for the life of the world. Christians are defined by our mission.

Now, firefighters have some limited dominion in our society. They have authority to inspect buildings for fire safety. They can determine legal occupancy for buildings. They must sign off on fire safety plans and can impose fines and penalties for violators. Firefighters can ignore certain laws. They can break speed limits and ignore traffic laws on the way to a fire or emergency. Firefighters have limited jurisdiction on scenes of accidents or fires. As public safety officers, they can tell us what to do in those situations and we are required to obey them. All of those parts of their vocation are based upon their mission. Their mission is to ensure public safety, and to preserve life and property, even if that means risking—or losing—their own lives in the process.

The Christian's role in society is analogous to that of the firefighter. The only difference is that we are not given any special authority by our society. We have no authority under the law. We are not allowed to break certain laws, typically, and we have no special jurisdiction. We cannot tell people how to behave, nor can we impose our beliefs on others. And yet our mission is to bear witness to the lordship of Jesus Christ, even if that means risking—or losing—our own lives in the process. The Christian mission is analogous to the mission of firefighters: the only difference is that we have to accomplish our mission without government-sanctioned power.

Governments promise a lot of things. Almost universally, they promise to provide their citizens with things like freedom, justice, and peace. Yet, we know those things actually originate with the story of God. Freedom, justice, and peace are themes that God has promised to accomplish on behalf of humanity. Governments constantly overstep their bounds because they have promised to accomplish what Christians believe only God can accomplish.

Only God can bring freedom, justice, and peace, which first and foremost come to us from the Scriptures. *Freedom* is the central theme of the Exodus narrative. The concept of freedom we find in the Scriptures teaches us that we are not slaves to sin, but we are free to be obedient to God. We are not to subject each other to slavery, but we are to recognize that each person is a precious child of God.

Justice is the theme of the prophets. Justice, in the Scriptures, is not about punishing the guilty, but about making sure that everyone has enough. Justice is about never letting wealth concentrate in the hands of the rich while the poor are starving.

Peace is the theme of much of the Bible. The Hebrew notion of peace is not a lack of war, but *shalom*, or the right ordering of all of life. Peace occurs when every part of each person's life is rightly ordered, including the way we relate to all other people and to the world itself.

Ultimately, freedom, justice, and peace are not national virtues: they are the virtues of the kingdom of God. The Christian's job is *not* to create a theocratic government through which we force people to live according to the virtues of freedom, justice, and peace because these things actually cannot come through power, control, and coercion. Power, control, and coercion destroy freedom, justice, and peace. These things come only through the cruciform life of discipleship.

Our job is to simply embody those things in the way we live our common life together. Within the life of the people of God— the church—we let freedom, justice, and peace reign as we lay down our lives for each other and for the world around us. This will produce in and through us a faithful witness to the reality that Jesus is Lord.

This is a profoundly political act. This is a faithful witness to the world. We do politics not primarily with our lips but with our lives. We are called to be a people of freedom, peace, and justice not through the exercise of power but through powerlessness; not through control but through self-sacrifice; not through coercion but through love.

We do politics the same way Jesus did—by patiently enduring suffering and persecution while living in faithfulness to the conviction that through Jesus, the future of God has broken into the present and is on the loose. This is how the kingdom comes. In the kingdom of God, up is down.

As a pastor, and especially as someone who teaches each week, I think that I may have one of the strangest jobs on the planet. Because our world works in a certain way, everybody knows the way the world works. There are rules: there is a structure, a pecking order. Everybody knows how the rules of the world work. Only the strong survive, right? Much of what I'm called to do as a pastor is to try to convince people that up is down, simply because Jesus said it was.

You will find your life by losing it.

You will lose your life trying to find it.

If you love someone, you must lay down your life for them.

If you have an enemy, you pray for them and love them.

In the kingdom of God, up is down.

DISCUSSION QUESTIONS

In what ways are we a part of the American "we"?

How does the idea of rejecting political party affiliation challenge you?

What do you think of the firefighter analogy for the church? Do you think it works? How have you experienced powerlessness?

How does your country promise to bring freedom, justice, and peace? How do the means of a nation differ from the means of the kingdom?

How will freedom, justice, and peace come through powerlessness, self-sacrifice, and love?

NOTES

Introduction

1. This is actually how the *New Revised Standard Version (NRSV)* of the Bible translates the passage.

Chapter 3

1. Walter Brueggemann, *Isaiah 40-66,* vol. 2, Westminster Bible Companion (Louisville, KY: Westminster John Knox Press, 1998), 193.

Chapter 4

1. Michael J. Gorman, *Inhabiting the Cruciform God: Kenosis, Justification, and Theosis in Paul's Narrative Soteriology* (Grand Rapids, MI: Eerdmans, 2009), 11.

2. Michael J. Gorman, *Cruciformity: Paul's Narrative Spirituality of the Cross* (Grand Rapids, MI: Eerdmans, 2001). The cruciform life is the focus of this wonderful book and is a consistent theme throughout Gorman's work.

Chapter 5

1. David Whitehouse, *Renaissance Genius: Galileo Galilei and His Legacy to Modern Science* (New York: Sterling, 2009), 87.

2. Rowan Williams, *Where God Happens: Discovering Christ in One Another* (Boston: New Seeds Books, 2005), 15.

3. Gordon Hempton and John Grossman, *One Square Inch of Silence: One Man's Quest to Preserve Quiet* (New York: Free Press, 2009), 13.

4. Stanley Hauerwas, *Working with Words: On Learning to Speak Christian* (Eugene, OR: Cascade, 2011), 84-85.

Chapter 6

1. Stanley Hauerwas, "The Tonto Principle," *Sojourners Magazine*, January-February, 2002.

JOURNEY THROUGH **PUBLIC JESUS** WITH YOUR COMMUNITY:

PUBLIC JESUS: SMALL GROUP EDITION
Exposing the Nature of God in Your Community

Includes 6 Video Sessions with Tim Suttle

To order go to thehousestudio.com

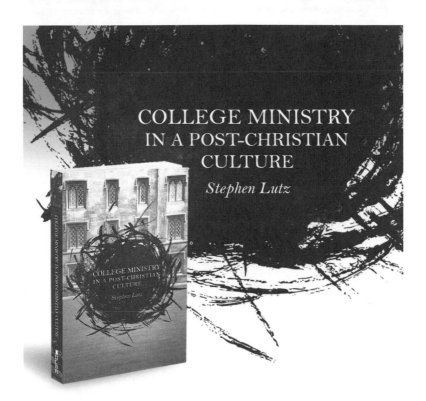

In *College Ministry in a Post-Christian Culture,* Stephen
Lutz translates missional theology to the practice of
college ministry—ministry as a proactive movement
that is constantly adapting to its ever-changing
environment. This resource will equip college ministry
staff, pastors, churches, and student leaders to minister
effectively to today's college students with both depth
and practical insight. Lutz walks readers through the
approaches needed to establish, grow, and
maintain a missional college ministry.

ECONOMY OF LOVE
Creating a Community of Enough

A Resource of Relational Tithe

Video Sessions with Shane Claiborne

In this five-week study, unpack what the patterns of God's kingdom look like compared to the patterns of our world. What is the value of enough, and how do we become more like the God who is close to the poor, the hungry, the meek, and the merciful?

Economy of Love will challenge individuals to join in community, journeying together as they begin to consider a new standard of living—a personal economic threshold oriented not around the size of a monthly paycheck, but around the value of enough.

To order go to thehousestudio.com